Never Give Up

My Life's Journey from the Markets to
the Big 'C' and Me

by

Keith A. Payne

Cover design, book build, Images, and
narration by: Marilyn Reid, Author/Illustrator,
Artspixels. Ltd., Unit 1 Cumberland Close,
Kirriemuir DD8 4EF Scotland U.K.

DEDICATION & ACKNOWLEDGEMENTS

In recognition to so many individuals who have stepped up to the plate, so to speak, I take this opportunity of giving a wholehearted thank you to those wonderful and amazing people who threw themselves into everything from sky-dives to home baking sales, in all covering over 30 fund raising events as well as recognising the tremendous personal financial donations made by so many individuals.

In March 2023 we set up the Big 'C' and Me Committee, made up of colleagues, to set out a schedule of fund raising events and to keep me in check. The committee members being drawn from the Morris Leslie Group's main head office, Caledonian House, Kinfauns. Thanks go to:-

H.R. Dept. Lianne Shannon, Graham Liddiard, Accounts Dept., Anna Wolski, Emma Smith Property Dept., Evelyn Havranek Design & Marketing Manager, Lee-Anne Wilson

Special thanks go out too, to the following individuals for their own fund raising events and for giving up their personal time and energy:-

Christine Torrie, Mandie Smith, Oksana Tracuma, Gary Howland and his team, Jackie Campbell - CHAS with her amazing team of volunteers.

Skydiving Team, 8 very courageous individuals, Anna Wolski, Oksana Tracuma, Jade Bloomer, Fraser Rolley, Andreja White, Ben Asensio, Ryan Townsley and Lee-Anne Wilson.

For donations toward the Big 'C' and Me with merchandise, their time and good will, Gregor Leslie, Steve Mason, Dawn Taylor, Monica Ziarcowska, Keith Merry, Ruiz Dalgliesh and Brandon Duthi.

My immediate family members, Keith Payne jnr., Jamie Payne, Shaun and Suzie Payne.

A very, very, special and deep hearted thanks goes towards Morris and Joyce Leslie, proprietors of the Morris Leslie Group. Graham Ogilvie, Groups Operational Director whose total support and individual encouragement is continually given towards myself and the Big 'C' and Me fundraising appeal.

Last but not least, a very special lady who has been my total bedrock throughout the Big 'C' Campaign, whose total enthusiasm, dedication and support is second to none, a very rare young lady indeed... there are some rare people in this world whose natural instincts are to put someone else's needs ahead of their own... those who offer encouragement when it is needed... who are always there to listen with a smile and a loving heart... who never expect praise for their good deeds because that's just the way they are... Lee-Ann Wilson you are one of those rare people.

I am so fortunate that you are not only a work colleague but, more importantly, a true and honest friend. Thank you.

Keith A. Payne, Errol, 2023

Chapter 1

In the beginning… 1882 – 1939

Over the past one hundred years, the beautiful north Cotswold village of Barton on the Heath has changed very little. Perfectly situated on a hillside from where it overlooks an agricultural landscape that spreads towards hills and valleys to the south, where Barton Hill dominates, the village lies a little north of its oldest building, the 13th century St. Lawrence Church.

Small, historical stone houses, with slate or stone tiles, surround the prominent triangular village green, but the largest, most dominating building lies north of the old church, and that building is the manor, known as Barton House, without which, this line of Payne's stories could not be told, for this is where their story began, in the Cotswolds.

Barton House is a grand stately home, built originally in 1200 AD, but only five vaulted cellars remain of that original build. The present Barton House was commissioned by one John Marshall whose family ran the estate for nearly a century from 1550, before it was handed over to the Overbury family in 1625. They put their stamp on it by having Inigo

8

Jones remodel the great hall, and install oak panelling in the Oak room, before settling down there for over one hundred and twenty years.

Next, came a family named Bird, who took over the estate in 1741. They were a wealthy silk merchant family from Coventry. It was this family's descendants who sold Barton House to Colonel Stanley Arnold in 1898, and he modernised it to suit his needs and then moved in with his family in 1901.

The Colonel had a lovely daughter whose name was Ethel Constance, and when he died, she inherited the beautiful Barton House, where she lived with her husband Robert Grosvenor Perry M.B.E., until the present family owners, the Cathie family, took it over in 1949.

The old estates in the United Kingdom tended to provide generations of families with a lifestyle of continuum, and this included life around the estates and in the villages attached to them. These English villages, little market towns, existed to provide the necessary tradesmen, produce, and workforce, required to keep such great estates running. Their grand homes required the best farms for produce, the best stables, and the best fields for horses and livestock. The owners hired estate farmers, blacksmiths, and stonemasons as well as domestic servants. The wives of all of these tradesmen working outside, usually worked inside the manor houses to keep them running smoothly.

Cooks, cleaners, matrons, nannies, an army of domestic staff, all performed the task of keeping Barton House in perfect tune, orchestrated by the Head Housekeeper, and often the Butler. Many generations of village working families served the needs of those residing in the "big house" in return for the continuum of a tied house and secure employment, and William Frank Payne was one such villager.

William was born in the market town of Barton on the Heath, and christened in the local church there, on the 27th August, 1882. At that time, Barton House was still owned by the wealthy silk merchant family, the Birds. When William grew up, his father passed on the family trade of stonemason to him, and young William probably accompanied him around the estate, working with his own father as he learned his trade on the job.

Eventually, William finished his apprenticeship and became employed himself by the Barton House estate, repairing and creating the many stone dykes, roofs, and buildings on the estate's farms, in its village, and of course, within Barton House and its environs.

Whilst working at Barton House, William met, and married, the love of his life, Sarah Annie Claydon, a local lass known to all as Annie. She was a domestic servant when they met. William and Annie remained living in the village as long as William was working at Barton House and there they had five sons and one little girl. Sadly, their darling daughter only lived until she was three years old. Her name was Daisy Isobel Payne. She passed over in May 1914.

Just three months before little Daisy's passing, Annie had given birth to another son, on the 6th of February, 1914, and it was this little son of William's who was destined to become the next estate stonemason at Barton house, after apprenticeship with his father. His name was Ronald Arthur Payne.

By this time, Colonel Stanley Arnold owned Barton House. All of William's five boys attended the local primary school in the village of Barton on the Heath. For them, their childhood was filled with happy freedoms in and around their beautiful village. There they heard exciting stories about William Shakespeare's aunt who once lived locally, and about characters from his plays, and of course their favourite stories about the adventures of the knights of old.

Ronald may have heard from William, whilst accompanying him around the estate, of how, the first ever Payne in England, who crossed the English Channel from France, was Hugh de Payns, the founder along with eight other knights who set up the "Knights of the Poor Fellow Combatants of Christ," whom we all know today as the Knights Templars.

Hugh de Payns first visited England about 1128. King Baldwin II of Jerusalem, his cousin, sent Hugh out on a mission across Europe to gain the support of influential noblemen, like himself, to help finance the Knights Templar order's stay in Jerusalem. He met with many knights, as well as kings and queens of the time. This is recorded in the Anglo Saxon Chronicle where it states:-

"This same year came from Jerusalem, Hugh of the Temple to the king in Normandy; and the king received him with much honour, and gave him rich presents in gold and silver. And afterwards he sent him to England and there he was received by all good men who gave him presents, and in Scotland also; and by him they sent to Jerusalem much wealth withal in gold and silver."

King Stephen and Queen Matilda gave many properties to Hugh de Payns, including an estate in Cressing in Essex in 1137. The barley barn the Templars built on that site still stands today, the oldest timber framed barn in the world.

Before long, the Templars developed new urban and rural settlements and market towns across England, Scotland, and Wales, and established residences and chapels. These new towns and villages were integral to the wider exploitation of rural resources.

The Templars had a significant impact on both rural and urban life in medieval England, which has been grossly underestimated. They introduced banking to the UK, market charters, they were even witnesses to the Magna Carta. They had economic bases in London, Warwick, Bristol, York, Lincoln, Chesterfield, Derby, to name a few, but their rural income overwhelmingly came from rural estates. They obtained grants for thriving market towns such as Wetherby, Whitham and Baldock, and other locations too. They were very effective and productive rural landowners and investors and all the market towns that they created benefited from the Templars economic know-how.

As soon as Ronald Arthur Payne left school, he began working alongside his father on the Barton House estate, gradually finishing his apprenticeship, and then he too was kept on as a full-time worker with the intent he would take over from his father William when he retired.

Just like his father before him, Ronald fell in love with a girl who worked in Barton House. This girl actually lived in at the house, she was the head housekeeper there and her name was Kathleen Eileen Smith, a dark-haired beauty from Wales.

Ronald was captivated by her. This girl was intelligent, independent, and a hard worker who had plans for the future. Not many girls in the village ever had the courage to leave home and work independently as Kathleen had.

On her days off, which would probably have been only once a month, Kathleen returned home to Wales to visit her mother in Bridgend, Glamorganshire. But any free time she had whilst on the estate after work, she began spending with Ronald. They would meet secretly at the little turret door tucked away near the back garden of Barton House, where neither their employers, nor their fellow workers, would see them.

Eventually, the loving couple formed a plan, after Ronald proposed to Kathleen, they decided that the next time she was off, he would accompany her to Bridgend to meet her parents and ask for her hand. They were married in Wales, at Bridgend on the 30th of April 1937.

On their return, they continued working at Barton House, but managed to find a cottage of their own in Little Wolford. Raven Cottage had no running water or electricity but to them it was a little paradise. They were now the happiest couple on the Barton estate.

At the time of Ronald and Kathleen's marriage, William was finding things difficult with his hands and as he was 55 years old his thoughts were turning to retirement. Years of lifting stones and roof tiles were taking their toll on him, so Ronald took on more and more of the heavier work for his father now that he was a fully qualified stonemason. He took pride in this work and he wanted to make his father proud of him.

For the next two years, life went on relatively normally in the sleepy, care-free village and estate, then on the 1st of April 1939, Ronald and Kathleen became the proud parents of a beautiful daughter named Maureen Valerie Gertrude. They were now a happy loving little family. Ronald could not have been prouder. Then, rumours began to circulate from the outside world in 1939. The Colonel was spending more and more time in London, and it was rumoured that conscription was being brought back for young men.

The second world war broke out in September 1939. Just two months later, in November 1939, young Ronald Arthur Payne aged 25 found himself enlisted and training with the Coldstream Guards preparing to go to war.

Chapter 2

Serving Others - 1941 to 1956

For Ronald Arthur Payne, the years between 1941 and 1943 meant hard training and discipline at the Coldstream Guards base where he was stationed at company headquarters. The Coldstream Guards became part of The British Expeditionary Force (BEF) in France when the second world war began, and they were already deployed in France.

Coldstream Guards are infantry soldiers, specialising in operations. They went from taking part in reconnaissance missions, to operating machine guns and mortars, as well as engaging with enemy troops on foot. Sometimes they used light vehicles.

This was a whole new world for young Ronald. At home in Barton on the Heath, his job as a stonemason had helped to keep him fit and strong, and whilst his army training was hard, he was categorised as very fit, an A1 category meant he was ready for battle abroad.

Before being sent abroad, he had been allowed some home leave to his beloved Kathleen early in 1942, and this re-union kept his little family close. Kathleen had fallen pregnant with her first son then, and they both agreed that she, and their daughter Maureen, should go and stay with Kathleen's mother, in Bridgend, Wales, while Ronald was away doing his duty.

In December 1942, their first son, Malcolm, was born in Ogmore Vale, Bridgend, Glamorgan. However, Ronald couldn't be there as his battalion was preparing for posting abroad. His girls and the new baby boy remained meantime with Kathleen's mother in Wales.

In August 1943, news finally broke that Ronald's battalion had to leave for North Africa. The Coldstream Guards had already suffered desperate losses and needed extra support. America had entered the war too, bringing much needed extra strength.

Once their enemies were defeated after several battles, the Coldstream Guards, were battle weary, exhausted, and psychologically affected by the terrible war scenes they witnessed in North Africa. With no time to recover, they were sent to Italy to fight Mussolini's fascists in what became known as the Italian Campaign. They didn't even have the right battle attire and spent the winter in Europe, in freezing, snowy conditions wearing the dress they had for North African weather. Conditions were dire.

The Italian Campaign was a huge effort to secure Europe. It lasted from September, 1943, until April, 1945, all told. 60,000 – 70,000 Allied troops died, and 100,000 German soldiers too. The final invasion of Sicily in July 1943 led to the collapse of the fascist Italian regime and brought about the fall of its leader, Mussolini, who was incarcerated on July 25th 1943. More than 150,000 Italian civilians were killed over that period.

British, American, Canadian, Albanian, Indians, French, Moroccans, Poles, New Zealanders, and more, formed the Allied Forces of which Ronald was a part. Many, many infantry soldiers were medically removed and sent home. Ronald was one of them.

He was medically boarded at Pinbright Camp from 15th April, 1944, having returned from the Italian Campaign in February due to his injuries. At Pinbright, the army declared him no longer fit for duties abroad and downgraded his medical category to a C2. Ronald was awarded the Italy Star medal for his bravery during the Italian campaign.

For a young man joining up to do his duty for King and Country, the reality of real war can shock them hard. World War 2 brought about such horrific scenes that many of those who returned refused to talk of such painful memories. Seeing those around you shot, blown up by mortars, and rescuing them from "no mans land," is hard for most of us alive today to imagine. Not to mention the atrocities they discovered there… Many of those actually involved in such scenes, fighting for their lives and ours, never spoke of their experiences later, and Ronald was one such soldier. But he was changed by these experiences, forever.

Although he healed from his physical injuries, his mental well-being, strength of coping with stress etc., was affected far longer and he was never quite the same. The army put him into ERE, extra regimental employment, home duties only, but he never quite picked up.

By the end of 1945 he was relieved of duty, put into a category C2 again, and the army sent him home on a long leave for 56 days to spend the Christmas of 1945 and the New Year of 1946, with his beloved Kathleen and their two children, in their little home at Raven Cottage, Little Wolford. By this time, Ronald and Kathleen's daughter Maureen was already attending the historical little primary school at Barton on the Heath, and Malcolm would soon be joining her there. Together again, they must have talked about their future. To be back in Barton on the Heath after the horror of the war he had just witnessed must have seemed overwhelmingly a relief for this brave country lad who had stepped up to the mark when requested to.

Now, returned to the woman he loved, Ronald was allowed a further six days leave with his family, until February 1946. Then the army released him of all full-time duties and popped his name on to the T/A Reserve list in case of recall, but for now, he could return home. Ronald was awarded two star medals, the Italy Star, the North African Star, and clasps, issued August 1948, and the Defence Medal 1939/45 for his gallantry.

Kathleen's husband was not the same young man who had left her at 25 years of age. Ronald was now a far more serious, mature 32-year-old man. But Kathleen never stopped loving him and they soon settled down to everyday life.

Ronald seemed more uneasy now, but he returned for a while to work at Barton House, walking to work from their cottage. He enjoyed collecting his children from the local village school in Barton on the Heath. Slowly this quieter life began to work on his well being and by 1953 they had even moved into a more modern house at number 2 Campden Close, Barton on the Heath. This lovely house with all mod cons was just what this growing family needed. Close again, they were delighted to discover that they were having a new addition to the family, and their second son, Keith Alistair Payne was born on the 4th July 1954, whilst they lived there.

Why Ronald left his employment at Barton House then, no-one knows. Perhaps he didn't get on with the new owners, who had taken over the house in 1949, the Cathies. Or perhaps they no longer required his services. It was about 1955, when Ronald took up his new position as a Scaffolding Erector, working for a company named Stanley F. Wass in Moreton in Marsh. The family moved again, to 3 Warwick Place, Shipton on Stour, to a lovely red bricked, three bedroomed semi-detached house with ample garden.

Kathleen and Ronald had just reached their early 40's by 1955, and young Maureen was about 16 and working in the local factory. This was the start of a new life. New job, new home, new town, new start. Maureen was a wonderful help to her mother with her baby brother Keith. Ronald even got himself a motorbike for travelling to work, much to the delight of their eldest son, the 11 years old Malcolm.

Another baby now, may not have been what Kathleen and Ronald needed, or expected, especially in their early 40's, but many pregnancies occur at that time in a woman's life, just before she will stop conceiving altogether. Kathleen and Ronald were no doubt amazed and felt blessed to discover that Kathleen was pregnant.

But this was a difficult one. The baby, thankfully, checked out healthy and normal for the relieved parents. The birth was traumatic for Kathleen and distressed Ronald immensely. Kathleen need to have a caesarean section to deliver her third son, Kevin Richard Payne, on the 21st August, 1956.

After her surgery, Kathleen was looking forward to seeing her husband and, tired though she was, she wrote a letter to her daughter Maureen who was looking after things at home for her. In her letter, she sent Maureen and Malcolm her love, and she asked Maureen to give her father Kathleen's lipstick so that Ronald could bring it to the hospital for her when he came up to visit. Ever organised, she wrote down exactly where it was, on the kitchen shelf. To everyone's shock and horror, Kathleen passed away just a few days after writing her letter.

Chapter 3

Coming to Grief - 1956 to 1959

To say that Ronald's world had just begun to turn upside down was more than an understatement. Every death, of someone close, causes a massive dynamical change to any family, it's true. But coming to grief for Ronald also meant losing his grip. The hardest hit, when coming to grief, are often those who have lost that certain someone in the family who took care of most of the domestic responsibilities. The war had already broken Ronald emotionally, and he had been plastered back together by Kathleen's love and security. He simply crashed, quietly, mentally. At that moment in time, surviving without Kathleen seemed, to him, an impossible consideration.

Kathleen had been head-housekeeper at Barton House when they first fell in love. She could organise. She could improvise. She could seek solutions and find them. They had lived through so very much, together. She ran their little family home beautifully, and efficiently. All Ronald had had to do was to go out to work and bring back his wages.

Ronald knew very little about budgeting, paying bills, or even how much things cost in the home. Kathleen did all of their housekeeping. She spoke proudly of being a housewife, because Ronald preferred her to stay at home and look after their home and their children.

His heart must have been smashed to smithereens when he kissed his poor wife Kathleen for the last time at the maternity hospital where she had just died and carried home his poor, motherless infant son, Kevin. Their home at Warwick Place was filled with relatives devastated and heart-broken over Kathleen's passing.

Her sister's hearts went straight out towards the children. Quite quickly, the women of the family decided to tackle the needs of the children. As capable as their beloved sister had been, they took charge, deciding that Malcolm now aged 11 should go and live with his Aunty Betty, (Mrs Ford), and uncle Raymond, who was a butcher, as she felt she couldn't manage a new baby. The Fords lived in Long Compton so it would be easy for Malcolm to visit home.

Their Aunt Dorothy, who lived in London, decided that she could look after baby Kevin, along with her husband Ron, and this would ease things for Maureen. The sisters understood how much Maureen had helped her mother Kathleen, now that she was 16-year-old, looking after her brother Keith, but to expect her to look after a new baby… That was far too much for a girl who had just lost her mother.

Meanwhile, Ronald, was in no fit state to make decisions about domestic arrangements for his family himself, so deep was his grief. Maureen agreed that she would look after her father's home and Keith, who was just past two when he lost his mother, until some day care could be arranged, as she had a little time off work for bereavement.

For the next few months, Ronald, having gone along with the women's plans, withdrew more and more. Robotically, he went to work, and then returned to the now, almost silent house. His father William was now poorly, and Ronald was worried about him too.

Meanwhile, Maureen tried her best to take care of the house, but her mother's death had left her heartbroken too. She went down to London to visit her Aunt Dot and Uncle Ron, to find out how her baby brother was doing and to take him out for walks because she wanted him to get to know her. She went over to Long Compton to see her brother Malcolm too, usually by herself. Everyone asked for her father but she just shook her head. Ronald would not engage with Maureen. She tried to talk to him about shopping etc., and occasionally he would hand her a pound or two. But he didn't seem to connect with her at all.

After about seven months of this lack of communication, Maureen exploded and told her father she was going back to work. It seemed to everyone who knew him, including Maureen then, that Ronald was just giving up on the rest of his family. She told him that her Aunt Dorothy was needing money if she was going to carry on looking after Kevin. Perhaps Maureen didn't realise that her Aunty Betty was also requiring money from her father, for looking after Malcolm.

One day soon afterwards, Ronald's troubled mind was going over the demands required of him for supporting his family at all of their different addresses, and he decided it would be less costly just to bring them all home. He couldn't even remember agreeing to these arrangements, but now he decided a housekeeper would be best. That way they could all be under the one roof again, where they belonged. The housekeeper could look after the little boys, Maureen could go back to work, and Malcolm could come home and finish his schooling.

Meanwhile Dorothy and her husband were finding things a bit difficult in London. She and Ron hadn't realised what the impact of having a baby in the house would have on them, or how costly a young baby can be. Dorothy was already 33 years of age and her husband, Ron, was 46. In the state of grief for her sister, Dorothy had been ruled by her emotions. She had made her decision to take baby Kevin with the best intentions, but she hadn't thought of the long term at all. Money was scarce, and Ronald couldn't provide them with any.

In January 1957, baby Kevin, now six months old, was returned to the care of his father and sister Maureen. That same month, Ronald's father William passed away, it was all too much for Ronald to cope with. He decided to write off to the Warwickshire Council Children's Officer and ask for help. He had been looking for housekeepers, but he couldn't give them a room of their own, nor could he afford one. He explained his lack of funds in his letter admitting he was so at a loss with worrying about the children, that he had been unable to eat and had lost 18lbs in weight. He ended his letter with, "…they are both as good as gold and I love them with all of my heart."

He fully intended to get temporary nursery help with the children until he could get back on his feet, and he stated that fact. He even asked for reassurance that they would be returned to him once he was working and earning again.

On the 27th May, 1957, little Keith and his baby brother Kevin, whom Keith had become very close to, were taken to the Grange Nursery in Myton, Warwick, and placed into residential care there, in response to their father's cry for help. Ronald was prepared to pay a parental contribution towards their care and the sum of money agreed with the Council for maintaining the children was fifty five shillings per week from May, and forty shillings per week from September 1957.

Ronald went back to work as a scaffold erector. His daughter Maureen contracted tuberculosis which was prolific after the war. The wages Ronald earned were pretty poor, and try as he might he could not make them stretch to paying the rent, the rates, the electricity and buying food for the home, as well as to the council's demands for maintenance. He had also become ill now, possibly with the stress, and certainly with a back injury, and this affected his work.

He finally found a housekeeper in September 1957, and wrote to the council again to inform them that after a few visits to the children he wished the children returned to him and both Keith and Kevin returned to Warwick Place and their father's care in October 1957.

Unfortunately, the housekeeper left the overcrowded conditions six months later.

By then, Ronald was worried sick again, and trying to pay off the arrears he had run up with the council. They were pressing him hard for their money. He had just written to them asking for them to reduce his payments as he was now paying for a housekeeper, when the housekeeper left. Maureen was not allowed to look after the children because she had had tuberculosis. Ronald was now in a fix.

A Children's Officer turned up at his work to talk to him on the 26th of April 1958, and he told her that his sister-in-law Mrs Ford, was going to help look after Keith and Kevin. The Children's Officer duly visited Mrs Ford, who gave an emphatic 'no' to the idea of her looking after the two little boys.

After listening to Mrs Ford, the concerned Children's Officer, went straight to Ronald's home at Warwick Place, to check out for herself who was looking after the children. She found Maureen at the home, preparing the children for bed at 5.45p.m. in the evening, she later reported. Maureen explained to the officer that she was expecting her father home around 7 p.m., that he ate out when working late. The officer promptly told Maureen that this was all very unsatisfactory and she removed the government family allowance book, the children's vitamin voucher book, and told Maureen someone would be coming to collect the children next day.

Ronald received this bad news when he returned home that night. The next day, 26th April, 1958, Keith and Kevin, were returned to the Grange Nursery, in Myton. That day, the Children's Officer was writing up her report.

She had been monitoring the family since the children had last been residing in the Grange. Before they returned to the Grange Nursery, she had already written out a letter to potential adoptive and foster parents regarding Kevin, on the 15th April, 1958. She wrote, "...there is the possibility of a little boy, born on the 21st of August 1956, coming into care at the end of the month. His mother died five days after his birth and his father has been trying to bring up his children with the help of housekeepers, but it has not been satisfactory and it is felt that if this little boy Kevin is to have the best chance of happiness, he should be adopted legally." One couple, Mr and Mrs Roberts, responded to receiving this letter from the Children's Officer, on 30th April, 1958, saying that they would like to meet Kevin and consider taking him instead of a new born baby. Kevin was fostered with Mr and Mrs Roberts with a view to adoption, on 10th May, 1958, just three weeks after leaving home.

Keith was very close to his little brother, especially since they'd already been sent away from home together. This created a deep bond of dependence between the two little boys. Keith had only been just over two years old at the time of his mother's passing, yet he'd had to deal with the deep hurt of missing her in an unhappy home filled with grief.

Both Kevin and Malcolm had been taken away to live with their aunts, whereas little Keith had to watch his father suffering grief, whilst struggling with his own two-years-old emotions, after losing the most important person in the world to him. At the Grange, now nearly four, he stuck to his little brother Kevin like glue, and he could not accept nor understand why his little brother was taken away from him by strangers, on 10thof May, 1958. He was so deeply traumatised by Kevin's departure, he had a really bad tantrum resulting in him fracturing his elbow. That night whilst two years old Kevin settled in to his new home, Keith slept in a hospital bed overnight after being treated under anaesthetic for his elbow.

On the 18th of May, 1958, Ronald was ill and off work from the engineering company he was now employed by, with a spinal injury. He wrote to the Children's Officer explaining how glad he was that Kevin was placed with foster parents and happy, as he himself was ill. He said he may consider adoption for Kevin, if it meant him receiving "the home comforts that mean so much to a child."

In early June, Ronald was referred by the council to the Magistrate's Court for arrears of maintenance payments. He could not pay as he was now on National Insurance benefit. The council sent back his family allowance payment book to him saying that he could send £2 per week from that. He replied to them in June, that he would be pleased to do so. Explaining that he had never been in such trouble with a magistrate before, he assured them that it would never happen again. The family allowance would go directly to the council officer to whom he was ordered to pay arrears to.

Ronald ended up in the Ellen Badger Hospital confined to bed with his spinal injuries. The Children's Officer arrived on the ward to visit him on the 10th of December, 1958, with a Justice of the Peace, to witness Ronald sign a paper agreeing for Kevin's legal adoption to begin. The forms had been sent to Ronald at the hospital.

In March 1959, Kevin was settling in well with Mr and Mrs Roberts, and at the Grange Nursery home, the matron wrote in a report, "Keith's mental progress greatly improved." It had taken Keith nearly a year to get over the separation from his little brother. Matron added, "…he fretted badly for sometime when his brother was adopted," and noted that he was just about ready for school.

Keith's father, Ronald, was on the mend in March 1959 too, and his mind was on his two little boys. At last, he was coming out of the veil of grief, back into the living world. He did not want to lose another of his sons. When he had had doubts about Kevin's adoption the previous June, he'd even considered marrying the housekeeper he had found at that time and mentioned to the Children's Officer he was thinking about bringing *both* his boys home. The reply from the officer said that, "As the child seems to be very happy, I suggest that you try to feel content in leaving him where he is…" Of course, that marriage proposal fell through… Kevin was adopted on the 24th of June, 1959, by Mr and Mrs Roberts.

Chapter 4

The Road to Hell is often Paved with Good Intentions - 1959 to 1969

The midsummer solstice of 1959, somehow brought Ronald sharply and clearly out of death's dimension and into the reality of his own life's challenges. Somehow the emotional impact on him of the finality of Kevin's adoption woke him up to the fact that he could also lose his other son, Keith. So, immediately after Kevin's adoption, Ronald was determined to get Keith home, somehow, and he wrote and told the Children's Officer, "…Keith would not be happy to call a foster father, "Daddy".

He and his eldest son Malcolm, who was now working, visited five years old Keith at the Grange over the next couple of weeks on their motorcycles. Ronald was back in work, feeling fitter, and getting stronger mentally again so he wrote to the council to tell them that he would be collecting his son Keith from them on the 23rd of July, 1959, just four weeks after Kevin's adoption.

Keith was delighted to be back home with his father. But the Children's Officer was still keeping an eye on the family when Keith was handed back to Ronald. Another home help/housekeeper had only lasted a couple of months so Ronald had arranged with Keith to be looked after every day, at first, by a neighbour who lived nearby.

This day care for Keith, provided by a lady just a few doors down the road, came to an end when the neighbour fell ill and suddenly went into hospital. The poor woman had informed the council who were supervising Keith's day care with her, so that day Keith was withdrawn from school and taken to another carer, Mrs Peace, who lived about two miles away, in Tredington.

Mrs Peace was also a registered foster carer and as Ronald had to do overtime, (he was still paying off arrears to the council until 1961), she agreed that Keith should stay with her during the week and return every weekend to his father. So, Joan Peace became Keith's foster mum and Ronald paid her faithfully.

By the following year, the resilient Keith had settled in perfectly to the routine of boarding out on school days and returning home at weekends. He struggled a little at school but his primary school head teacher noted in June 1960 that he was a "happy little boy who tried hard with his work and co-operated well with others.

Meantime, Ronald, determined to get the Children's Officer out of their lives completely, finally paid off the debt he owed them, in 1961. His intention, at that time, was to take a wife and to get Keith back home permanently. The woman he chose to marry, was named Eileen. She was Welsh, like his first wife. But that was where the resemblance ended.

After their marriage, Eileen moved in with Ronald, along with her young son from a previous marriage, Gareth, to Ronald's home at Warwick Drive. In March 1961, Keith returned home to live with his father and step-mother full-time. He was seven years old.

Before long, Keith began struggling at school. His headmaster, during his last term at his primary school wrote that Keith was "struggling but progressing." He was struggling at home too. The good intentions of his father, to provide a home with a "mother" in it so that Keith could have a "normal" family home, were no way reflected by his wife Eileen. She simply saw Keith's return as more money staying in the house instead of paying for him being looked after. Affection did not come into it.

Ronald's life with Eileen reverted to the same routine he had had with his first wife. He dutifully went to work, and every week, he handed up his wages to his wife to enable her to manage the housekeeping, pay bills etc. This was a relief to Ronald and he happily passed all domestic responsibility over to Eileen.

To assist with the expense of food bills, Ronald also worked hard in his large garden growing the fruit and vegetables needed to help feed his growing family. He was an excellent gardener and pretty much self-sufficient. He was content for the first time in years. He never spoke of the past. Not of his war years, nor about his first wife Kathleen, not even about Kevin, to Eileen. He had learned to live in the moment and that way he coped better with life. This suited Eileen who adapted quickly, and took control of both the house and all of those residing in it, including Keith. She had a strong character, and a bitter tongue, and Ronald and Keith were often lashed with it if they upset her in any way.

On Ronald's only day off work, Sunday, Keith often lay in bed listening to Eileen and his father's raised voices as they argued about many things, often about how useless Ronald was, but mostly about money. She wanting more, he accusing her of squandering and getting them into debt. These arguments often ended in Ronald dashing upstairs and him storming into Keith's bedroom, commanding him to get out of bed as they were going out, leading to Keith happily clinging on to his father's back as they sped off on his motorbike to the Mallory race course.

In front of Ronald, Eileen tolerated Keith. Behind Ronald's back, she was cruel to Keith who tried to please her by making her proud of him. He did a paper round at five in the morning from the age of 11 to contribute to the family income she was always shouting about.

No matter the weather, she would send Keith out to dig up vegetables even in the frostiest and wettest of nights, and when she wanted him to peel potatoes for her, he felt sick to the stomach about doing that chore because he realised quickly that he could never peel them right for her, and would be verbally or physically abused by her whilst carrying out the task.

This type of cruel treatment is often dished out to children living in foster care and/or children's homes. It is very confusing and emotionally damaging for them as it is a type of bullying that has no reasoning other than their actual existence. Children in foster care often suffer such cruel attacks of such bullying from foster siblings, and/or from one/other or both of their foster parents, being a cuckoo in the nest so to speak. No matter how hard they try, these poor children cannot win over such jealousy, neither will they ever be able to please those who feel so negatively about their actual presence… and step children too are often treated the same way.

Keith's attempts to please his step-mother never worked and her hateful treatment continued especially when he was alone with her, when she would verbally and sometimes physically assault him. His father was also bullied by Eileen, but he knew how to escape her lashing tongue. The Sundays that he took Keith with him for the whole day to the Mallory race course, were some of the best days of young Keith's life. Wonderful, "golden nugget days" that Keith would never forget.

This iconic motor sport course, nestled within the very heart of Leicestershire, was the perfect escape for Keith and his father. Mallory Park's location amongst tranquil hills and lakes, welcomed its visitors and even inspired them to participate, as well as spectate.

Keith and Ronald, sat high up upon the grass bank opposite the start/finish line, where the view allowed them to see the majority of the circuit. Some of these thrilling racing experiences allowed young Keith to see the likes of Mike Hailwood, Giacome Agostini, Phil Read, and other top international riders.

While father and son, happily shared these racing experiences, they shared the picnic Ronald had brought for them from home, marmalade sarnies and home-made cakes. Keith hugged his father all the way home as he held on during the bike ride home. Exhilarated by the day's events, both of their hearts would calm down a little during the ride home knowing that they were about to face the wrath of Eileen, but for now, the love, excitement, and unspoken understanding of this special time spent together was all that mattered.

In 1965, Keith was enrolled at Shipton High School, and he and his father proudly posed for a photograph. All told, his father felt grateful that they were at least part of a family again. But Keith did not share his father's acceptance of this new family quite so well. During the past few years, Keith's step-mother had given birth to two little boys. Things were crowded at home and money was short as usual. Keith felt just as much a cuckoo in the nest in his own home, as he would had he been fostered, Eileen's own children's needs being her priority. She refused to buy him the long trousers he required for starting high school, insisting that he wear short trousers, which to Keith, was another humiliation.

Eileen and Ronald intended moving to a larger house in Shipton on Stour, and to make ends

meet, Eileen had been making small payments
to a weekly shopping catalogue. She told Keith
he'd have to start paying for his own clothes if
he needed any, as she would have to order them
from her shopping catalogue.

Now to many young teenagers, this might have
seemed an impossible task, but Keith came
from strong, determined stock. He would find
a solution. Already working on his paper round
in the early mornings, he looked for another
job, after school. Ronald was now working in a
factory in Shipston-on-Stour, and they were
about to move to number 7 Mayo Road in that
town, so Keith found himself a job working for
the local grocer. He would pack up grocery
orders in the evenings, and do deliveries with
the van on Saturdays. He triumphantly told
Eileen that he could now order his long
trousers, white shirts, and sports clothing, all of
which he required for high school.

Keith was now working seven days a week,
before and after school, and he struggled
through the first couple of years at high school.
In 1966, every man in England required some
new technology… a television. England was in
the world cup final and everyone wanted to
watch it on television. Ronald too, was
determined to have a t.v. Eileen hired one
where coins had to be inserted to view.

About the same time, Eileen's behaviour was becoming so intolerable, that Keith decided to run away. One day after a ramification with her, Keith walked the two miles to the home of his previous foster mother, Joan Peace, and asked to stay there. Mrs Peace had to inform the authorities, and they interviewed Eileen and Ronald about the situation at home and the treatment Keith had been receiving there. Keith was returned home, and now that his father knew how bad things had been between Keith and Eileen, things at home improved a little. Eileen and Keith simply tolerated one another.

His jobs kept him out of Eileen's way and during the school holidays Keith, like most working-class kids around the U.K. at that time, found himself doing some kind of agricultural work to help farmers and boost family incomes. They did everything from picking fruit to hay-stacking, and reselling barrowloads of black currants to the local greengrocer in summer, to picking potatoes, apples, and chestnuts in the autumn. Occasionally they were rewarded with a sixpence to visit the local cinema after handing up most of their pay. Working meant Keith was hardly at home, spending less time with Eileen.

After a rocky start at the Shipston High School, Keith struggled through the first couple of years

there. However, as soon as he reached third
year, he was doing so well and improving in all
subjects, he climbed from form position 24 to
position 11. His improvement had begun in
year two, where in the 2nd half of term he
began to progress. Perhaps he knew that if he
wanted to get anywhere in the world, this last
year in school would matter. Young Keith was
turning into an independent young man who
had plans for the future.

As soon as he could, Keith left home to become
independent completely, and in 1969 he found
himself enlisted in the army stationed at the
Junior Infantry Battalion, Sir John Moore's
Barracks, Shorncliffe, Kent. Happy to leave
home behind, he quickly adapted to the robust
and disciplined routine the army gave him.

The tentacles of his controlling step-mother
reached out to Keith even then, in the form of
letters demanding money, for the never-ending
shopping account. Keith received three letters
over a period of just three weeks insulting him
and demanding money from him from a
monthly salary he hadn't even had time to
receive. He organised an advancement of his
wages to send payment to her.

By the time Keith went home on his first leave,
he had grown in confidence and wisdom. His
combined childhood experiences had given him

a lot of insight into human beings, insights that many people take years to discover. He was developing fast into a young man equipped with the social skills needed to cope with people out in the wider world. The first person he dealt with, when he went home on that first leave from the army was Eileen.

All children grow up, and those who treat them badly ought to remember that. Keith was confident enough by that age to find the courage to confront the jealous bully that she was, and to confront her about her dreadful behaviour towards him and his father over the years. He was never subjected to any threatening behaviour from her again, and now, more than ever, Keith was ready to look after himself.

Chapter 5

Freedom to Be - 1971 to 1973

When Keith left the British Army after 18 months service in 1971, his commanding officer wrote "Tall, smart and intelligent, Payne would have made a good soldier. He has shown initiative and leadership, and should do well in work he enjoys." Freedom called and the world was his oyster. Uncertain of exactly where he wanted to go in life, he knew that freedom and independence could only come by determination and hard work and, since he'd always loved cooking, Keith had visions of becoming a world class chef.

So, after settling into a nearby caravan park in Stratford upon Avon, Keith began working as a trainee chef at a local restaurant called "The Golden Egg."

Golden Egg restaurants were about a "fun eating experience" and they were extravagantly furnished and lit. By the time Keith joined the restaurant in Stratford Upon Avon in 1971, a franchise run by his French born employer Georgette, there were over 40 restaurants in the Golden Egg chain, and they had even opened one restaurant in Scotland. The chain had only just been sold to J. Lyons when Keith's cooking apprenticeship began.

The quirky dining décor of Golden Egg Restaurants was often jazzily complimented with brilliant coloured lighting. Even today, many people remember the large menu presented to them in the shape of a giant golden egg and their distinct designs are still discussed in design schools. A completely different working atmosphere for Keith compared to the conservatism of army life. However, the discipline in the army had taught him to be steadfast when learning new skills, and although he worked long hours for an extremely low wage, the Golden Egg was to become a path presenting other opportunities for him.

Keith's father, Ronald, was working in a nearby factory at that time that manufactured pots and pans. Ronald and his fellow workers took a company bus to work and back. Travelling on the way back home from the factory, the workers' bus would pass the Golden Egg restaurant and so Keith would try to stand outside of it to wave to his Dad if it happened to pass by during his shift.

Just one year later, in 1972, whilst staying over at a girlfriend's parents' house, Keith was introduced to a man named Nigel Maby and his first wife, Penny, who were also visiting the girl's parents. Nigel had just formed a new and ambitious general retail market operating company. This company was named "Spook Erection", and it was destined to become a dynamic, pioneering, profitable, and adventurous private markets operator.

Nigel and Keith shared a drink or two and Keith was impressed by Nigel's vision and reasons for bringing back trading markets to towns in England. Especially to those that had been built originally for just that purpose, as "market towns". New shopping centres were being erected in many towns where markets had once had pride of place. Keith felt inspired by listening to Nigel.

Nigel was impressed by Keith's interest and keenness about his new company and his excellent instincts told him he could trust Keith. So, he offered him the opportunity to come and work with him and his company, Spook Erection, where he could learn all about market trading. The work would be hard, long hours, outdoors mostly, with strict rules but with excellent monetary reward. To Keith it was a "no brainer".

Just one week later, Keith was in Moreton in Marsh where Nigel was based. Nigel had a cottage in Moreton in Marsh and he ran his company from a yard on British Rail land nearby. After a long interview Keith accepted Nigel's offer and moved in temporarily with his sister Maureen and her husband and their daughter Tracy, to be closer to the yard.

Nigel himself had traded in linens and textiles from market stalls provided by Warwick Council, who raised and dismantled them. At the beginning of forming his company in 1968, Nigel had agreed to do this for the council at Warwick and, from this early beginning, Spook Erection was born and expanded to supply stalls and services to general retail markets. Nigel's company name came about from the nickname he had gained reflecting his ability to erect complete outdoor markets after midnight as quietly as possible in the market square or site concerned.

Spook Erection's system of working meant that any man could begin work for them as a labourer and work their way up, from making and market stalls in the yard, then on to market sites collecting rents for stalls and pitches, to becoming a Superintendent, or "Toby" as they're known in the market trade. On his first day at the offices of the Spook Erection enterprise, Keith was amazed when he saw his first market with Nigel Maby, which was a Sunday Market located on the outskirts of Melton Mowbray on a WWII airfield.

At First Keith learned the yard work... how to weld, size, and paint stalls with red lead paint. The first market he was ever involved with running for Spook Erection was the market of Southwell in Nottinghamshire on a Saturday. Keith and another worker would travel up there on a Friday morning, erect the market and run it on the Saturday. It was an excellent grounding for Keith, who was only 19 years of age at the time. Once the Saturday market was over, Keith and his fellow worker would get back to Melton Mowbray in time for the Sunday market there where Keith was now assistant rent man.

Rules dictated what could and couldn't be sold on Sundays and Trade and Standards Council employees could turn up any time to make sure a market was going by these rules... and Nigel's company rules for traders had to be treated with just as much respect.

It was during his early occupation at Southwall market that Keith had the first of his occasional run-ins with Nigel and he never forgot it! It was a cup final day and as the rain was pouring down, Keith had taken to the inside of his van to listen to the cup final on the radio. Many traders had already packed up early due to the weather. Nigel turned up unexpectedly and when he saw that traders were leaving early, he went looking for Keith and when he found him in the van he was furious. He ordered Keith out of the van and ordered him to make the traders who were still around set up again. If he didn't he'd be out of a job! Nigel stuck to the rules of his company, and he expected everyone else to do the same. But he did not keep up a grudge, and he and Keith were soon firm friends once more.

After organising and working car parking and labouring at Melton Mowbray for a number of months, Keith was asked to accompany the General Foreman for England and Wales, as the company were opening another market in Yorkshire on a Sunday, at Melbourne. The two men spent a lot of time working together and Keith helped to get that market site ready. This market was quite quickly shut down by the local authority but the experience working it was invaluable to Keith. Another, regular job Keith did on Sundays was to take cash collected at Melton Mowbray Sunday market to Spook's offices at Moreton-in-Marsh to enable wages to be made up for Spook employees when they arrived back to base after the Melton Mowbray market.

By 1973 the company had expanded across the Cotswolds and into other towns so that teams of men were erecting and dismantling markets seven days a week. In November 1973, the Walsall Observer reported how the traders at

Brownhills market were optimistically looking forward to the new year after their first successful year and how Spook Erection were controlling 25 markets then including Brownhills and the fast-growing Tewkesbury that Nigel had opened in 1971. They also reported how the company's logo had been changed into a pregnant ghost to reflect its continual expansion.

By this time Spook Erection had about 12 vans, each with the Spook Erection pregnant ghost company logo painted on it, and work for Keith began at 4am. Next, they expanded into Wales, opening outdoor markets at Newport and Blackwood, as well as an indoor market at Brecon Beacon.

It was also in 1973, when Keith was only 19 years old, that Nigel set his sights upon Scotland and he had Keith in mind to accompany him. Keith had proven to Nigel that he was a reliable and capable employee and Nigel was about to reward him for that by putting him in charge of what would become the largest market in the U.K., at Ingliston, near Edinburgh.

Market mania hits Ingliston

The Golden Egg

Chapter 6

Freedom to Be - 1973 to 1978

Just five years after its founding, Spook Erection was developing and growing fast, and Keith along with it. For the first time in his life he felt in control of his own destiny and security. Nigel's company motto, "Where Knowledge Flows, Prosperity Grows," was one he believed should be applied to any business, not just the market retail trade. Wisely, he knew that the success of Spook Erection could only happen with teams of good people who knew what the company rules were; those who implemented them; and those who knew where to find advice should problems arise. He wrote up booklets and flyers to guide both employees and traders, all of which were printed at the company headquarters in Moreton-in-Marsh.

Both indoor and open-air markets have certain ancient and modern laws attached to them. Nigel knew that his company wouldn't last long without strict adherence to these rules. He was up against many large retailers who did not want small trades taking business from them, as well as councils who had long forgotten the ancient rules of markets and fairs. He had to be sure about what he was doing during his company's expansion. So, he shared his marketing know-how with both employees and the traders who rented pitches from his company, knowing that their success or failure could indirectly mirror his.

This was vital to the success of all concerned because not only did the local council trading rules have to be considered but also the national laws of all four nations of Britain. It was whilst considering these that Nigel Maby realized that Scottish law in relation to markets, compared to English law, could benefit his business.

The evolution of market towns in Britain and their expansion from the 10th to the 13th centuries ultimately led to the rules and regulations governing the level of impersonal and large-scale trade occurring in modern economies today, but they originate from the far more personal contact of communities and local trades.

In earlier days, both pillar stones and market crosses were the places where communities would gather to sell their wares, hear news and even to see punishments served out to offenders by way of wooden stocks, sometimes even whipping posts. Those trading outside market areas and trading times were heavily punished.

The ancient market rights of England originally established on the Magna Carta of 1215, as witnessed by the Knights Templar order, (who created many market towns themselves), were later incorporated into the statute of Fraudulent Conveyances of 1677. The plague of 1665 and the great fire of London in 1666, both led to this change in market laws after an Act of Parliament in 1674 banned trading within the city walls. This act led to Britain's most historic markets, Petticoat and Brick Lane markets, being moved outside the walls of the city to where they still stand today and remain a prominent part of London culture after 400 years.

These changes had a lasting effect on modern markets, particularly in relation to the concept of "stewardship", where a company or individual has the responsibility of ensuring that goods and services are purchased and sold in a fair and honest manner, in accordance with the laws and they also apply to the shopkeepers who began to replace markets. In modern day markets, the concept of stewardship is incorporated into the Fair-Trading Act of 1986. The person for implementing these rules and regulations, and keeping Traders' right, was known as "the Toby".

The Toby organised the allocation of pitches at market sites, and was responsible for collecting rents, as well as directing teams who were dismantling and erecting stalls. It takes strength of character, nerve and determination to deal with all of the complexities of traders. The Toby had to earn the trust and respect of them all to be able to do his job.

Rules and regulations also differ according to the type of trading and these could cause upset. For example, charitable traders, such as those who became the Pearly Kings and Queens of Petticoat Lane Market in England paid no rent so were not always welcome because other traders resented them for stealing their trade. Such charitable traders were known as "costers" or "costermongers" and they became protected by law in 1894, after which they copied the dress of Harry Croft, the street sweeper who founded them and who wore pearl buttons manufactured in east end factories. There were rules for everyone trading whether they were an artisan shoe maker whose leather had to be stamped and authorised by a "leather sealer", or a beer seller whose trade depended upon the judgement of an "ale conner".

The markets were arising like phoenixes across the U.K., resurrected by Spook Erection in the 20th century. So, in 1973 Keith found himself travelling with an articulated lorry carrying 100 stalls, accompanied by another lad, Fred Walker, to Scotland to set up Spook Erection's first Scottish market at Ingliston, just outside Edinburgh.

On that first July market day, they operated with 100 stalls and Nigel's original intention was to have up to 120 units. However, the demand for stalls quite quickly rose, so an extra 80 stalls per week began being delivered to Ingliston. The adjoining car park soon had to be expanded into a neighbouring field to accommodate the number of trading stalls arriving on site.

Traders from Nigel's other markets in England soon began travelling up from places like Newcastle, Preston, and even Birmingham, to trade at Ingliston, and their Scottish customers welcomed them. Indoor markets and arcades had existed in Scotland in the 1970's such as the Barrowlands in Glasgow, and the Dens Road Market in Dundee. The last time Dundee had seen an open air market was from the days of Queen Victoria when the Greenmarket was operating there until the about 1934 after moving three times for demolition to allow the Caird Hall to be built, and the community memory of the old markets, still held dear to the hearts of the people, ensuring a great welcome for the open air market at Ingliston, and they soon flocked to it from all over Scotland.

It wasn't long before the success of Ingliston meant that the company had to move it to a larger, second location about half a mile away after negotiations with The Royal Highland Society who owned the grounds. For Keith, life was now a non-stop commute between England and Scotland, and hard work seven days a week.

Keith's new roles of responsibility kept him busy, and he and his teams of workmen worked hard and played hard. They often enjoyed time in the local pubs after working all night setting up market stalls, wherever they might be. Life is for living, and Keith was living life to the full. His social skills were second to none. Being placed into the wider world and experiencing a variety of social situations as he did in his childhood, Keith instinctively learned more than most about human nature, and his army training had brought out a confident independence in him.

Privately, he had built up a good relationship with his father and reconnected with his sister Maureen and brother Malcolm and he would catch up with them all when he was home. But he had lost all recollection of his brother Kevin. The grief he had suffered as a child when separated from Kevin had caused Keith to completely erase the memories of their shared childhood from his own mind and since

Kevin's adoption no-one, not his father Ronald nor his step mother Eileen, or even his sister Maureen, had ever mentioned Kevin, or what happened to him whilst Keith was growing up. So, Keith was unaware of Kevin's existence, but getting along with his family reasonably well.

Whilst pursuing his career in the market trade, his childhood experiences seemed very far away to Keith and life for him was feeling good when he fell in love and married the woman who was to became his wife and the mother of his children, Theresa.

Theresa Rose was working, helping a trader on the markets working on behalf of a man who sold fashion wear in the Barrows, Glasgow. When she and Keith first met she was bunking off school trading at Airdrie for this trader. A Scottish lassie, she was from the east end of Glasgow. Theresa came from a large, strong proud Glaswegian family and lived with her mother, grandmother, sister, and four brothers in a tenement in Glasgow. She and Keith had tied the knot at Tollcross Glasgow on the 1st of February in 1975, and on the 19th May in Edinburgh, Theresa gave birth to their first child, a son named Keith Richard Payne. Keith now felt like the proudest man on the planet.

Meantime, Nigel was testing the watery laws of marketing down south in Wellesbourne where local laws allowed him to operate a week day market on 14 occasions without planning permission. He opened it on the 2nd of April, 1975 to some hostility. The Coventry Evening times reported that the chairman of the Parish Council was calling for a boycott.

Nigel's attention took a different direction in 1976 when he was excitedly arranging the transportation from England to Scotland of a work of art he intended erecting permanently at Ingliston. Meantime, Keith was concerned with matters much closer to home. Theresa was about to give birth to their second child, a daughter named Annamarie, who was also born in Edinburgh.

Keith could not be happier, but because of his extra ordinary work hours, Theresa went home with her children then to spend some time with her mother in Glasgow, then on Keith's return, they purchased a mobile home on a site in Loanhead, Edinburgh.

He had proved himself to Nigel and Keith's hard work paid off. So much so that by the age of 21 he was Manager at Airdrie, Musselborough, and Bonnyrigg, as well as Ingliston. Keith was also proud of being a happily married father of two.

Chapter 7

Kings and Empires - 1976 to 1979

By 1976 Keith was on top of the world thoroughly enjoying his fast, hard working life, and Nigel Maby seemed to have the "Midas Touch". His company, Spook Erection, was growing in wealth, he was continuing to erect more and more open-air markets across the country and Ingliston was the jewel in his crown and he was proudly driving a Rolls Royce with the number plate SE 1. The company's main office was still based in Moreton-in-the-Marsh where Nigel was based himself for the majority of the working week but that was changing as he visited Scotland more and more.

Whilst in Scotland in 1976, Nigel had a suite in the Royal Scots Hotel in Edinburgh and as his expanding businesses grew in Scotland he would often fly back and forth between north and south, so it wasn't long before he was looking at property to set up a new home in Scotland for himself. In August that year, Nigel purchased the work of art that was to become synonymous with Ingliston, created by the British sculptor, Nicholas Monro, an 18ft gorilla modelled on the fictional giant gorilla, King Kong.

The King Kong statue was originally commissioned in 1972 for display in Manzoni Gardens, in The Bull Ring in the centre of Birmingham, for display from March to November as part of a Sculpture in Public Places Scheme in 1972, in partnership with the Arts Council of Great Britain. When that scheme ended, King Kong was purchased by a car dealer where it stood for four years as a publicity tool until Nigel purchased it in 1976 for £12,700, and transported it to Scotland to take pride of place at Ingliston Market where it was to stand for over 30 years.

Soon after, Nigel Maby found a property in Scotland, quite near to Ingliston market. This property consisted of two bungalows which were joined together to make one larger home for Nigel, enclosed in eight acres of ground. Nigel's home was called "Ingliston Castle" and it soon became his home/office in Scotland.

The King Kong fiberglass work of art somehow blended in perfectly with the happy atmospheric bustle and magic excitement of the market at Ingliston and was an unforgettable icon for visitors. It became a meeting place, a talking point, and a great promotional tool for Spook Erection.

By this time, Ingliston had expanded again into a grassy field and there were over 800 semi-permanent fixed stalls with only two workers, Keith and another man to set it all up. The field was on a slope however, and straw bales were constantly necessary for the sodden ground after rainfall.

The rapid growth and development of Ingliston prompted Nigel to discuss and plan with Keith the opening of an indoor market in Edinburgh around 1977. Perhaps Nigel thought that this would curb the growth of Ingliston somewhat before it became too big to handle.

Along with his other markets in Scotland, Nigel had also opened one at Airdrie Football Club, which ran on a Tuesday, and Keith and Fred Walker would erect that on a Monday then dismantle it the same night to travel back down to Moreton in Marsh for a few days off. By 1977 the company were operating 20 week-day and weekend markets in Scotland including Hamilton, Blantyre and Wishaw. It was an extremely hectic period, but a continual learning curve for Keith.

Altogether, Nigel was now operating about 50 markets up and down the country. They were trading on different days of every week, and all of them required erecting and dismantling. His empire and employee numbers were growing fast.

About the same time as the Edinburgh Central indoor market at Lothian Road was being created, Nigel was negotiating with Kirkcaldy Council in Scotland regarding establishing an open-air market there according to its ancient charters. On the 9th of November, in 1977, Nigel had a telephone conversation with Mr Douglas Nelson, the Kirkcaldy Council's director of planning at that time. He was asking him what progress had been made in relation to his request to open a market site in the town and he was told his request was under consideration. He replied to the director, "You will get a surprise one of these days."

Nigel was already unhappy with Kirkcaldy District Council because when he had set up in Kirkcaldy previously at premises in Balfour Street, the deal was terminated and then he had moved to Volunteers Green. This was an open grass area historically granted to the people of Kirkcaldy and Kirkcaldy District Council had forced Spook Erection out of there.

That Friday, a civil action was raised at Kirkcaldy Sherriff Court by one of Nigel Maby's employees claiming that, by Royal Charter, a market should be held every Saturday in the town. Direct action was taken on Saturday 12th November, 1977, when a convoy of vehicles, reportedly 100 vans, headed into the town centre led by Keith and Nigel Maby in his Rolls Royce, at 7.10 a.m. When they reached the old Forth Road Bridge which had a toll fee then, Keith paid the tolls for all of the vehicles before they were waved along.

The police were called when the convoy was noticed driving towards Kirkcaldy. The convoy stopped in the High Street and started to set up market stalls. Once set up, the market stalls stretched from the Mercat to Port Brae. There was no way through for traffic and the street was closed until about 11a.m., creating chaotic conditions for pedestrians as well as traffic problems. Apparently, the stalls were blocking shop doorways and exits as well as sitting above fire hydrants!

The traders tried their best to ignore the Police when they arrived but some of them packed up and left. All seven who refused were arrested, along with Nigel and Keith, and they spent the weekend in custody before appearing at Kirkcaldy Sheriff Court.

They were charged with committing a breach of the peace by refusing to remove their stalls, and with conducting themselves in a disorderly manner, to which they all admitted. A Mr

Brian Wood represented them in court. He told the court that the Royal Charter did indeed make provision for a street market in Kirkcaldy, to be held every Saturday, and on certain other days of the year for the benefit of the Burgh and its inhabitants. He also stated that the traders had got up a petition with 9,800 names of support.

Nigel was fined £150 and the traders who came from Clydebank, Wishaw, Edinburgh and Kirkcaldy were fined between £35 and £65. Keith was fined £65 for organising the invasion, which was paid for by Spook Erection. After his appearance in court, Nigel said that the market stunt was a frustrated cry against the council. He did not feel it was a wasted trip because he felt, as he said at that time, "Traders should have had the opportunity to sell their goods. The least we have done is bring the matter into the public eye, and into the eye of Kirkcaldy District Council which must now realise it has to do something constructive."

These events were also discussed later at a meeting of the council's sub-committee. With feathers ruffled, Cllr James Brodie said it was "diabolical" that outsiders could come into town and cause such chaos.

There were no indoor markets in Edinburgh when Nigel decided to operate one there. This would be his first – and last – venture into indoor markets. Since Ingliston was such a success, he felt the traders he already had would be interested in trading there, so he obtained an old "Grant's" department store located on Lothian Road in Edinburgh that consisted of three floors for the purpose.

The idea was that traders could build their own stalls in the building. Some of them invested their money in splendid stalls and before long there were 250 traders on the three floors making the place fully occupied from day one. The units looked incredible and Keith and his team ripped out the glass frontage windows along the stores frontage and replaced them with roller shutters on two sides of the building so that the whole of the front was open. A flat was even built into the indoor market for Keith and to stay in whilst there.

On the back of Ingliston's fame, when the people of Edinburgh heard about this new indoor market, they queued all day to get in. The place was packed with customers the first day. Then the following day, two men arrived bearing writs from the Edinburgh City Council demanding to see Nigel Maby. Keith was ordered to close the building down within the hour as it was a fire risk due to the high volume of footfall.

In order to comply, Spook Erection built fire escapes and altered anywhere in the building that the council said did not fit their rules. After being closed, and complying to every building rule thrown at them by the council, they were told the stalls did not comply with the rules. All the stalls had to be painted with fireproof paint and six months later, when the market re-opened the brightly painted, exciting indoor market design looked nothing like before. There was so much adverse publicity attracted by it all the momentum from the public had gone and after 18 months the entire venture failed and closed down.

Nigel decided to concentrate on creating a beautiful garden in the grounds surrounding his Scottish home by rerouting a stream that flowed through it and building a beautiful rock garden. It was there he once created an island habitat for rats, surrounded by a moat, where he kept 200 white rats who were fed on garbage from Ingliston. The more public one's life becomes, the more private one's home has to be in order to keep a happy and healthy mind, and Nigel was keeping himself and his business more and more close to home as it grew.

The Scottish office for Spook Erection was based at Lochend, Newbridge, not very far from Ingliston and Nigel's staff there consisted of Fred Coutts, who became a Manager, Alan Ford; an architect, Graham MacDonald, Foreman, Bob Hendry, Placement Officer and Erica Steadmand and Julie Coventry, Secretarial duties. Nigel himself, preferring by this stage to work from his home at Ingliston Castle.

By 1978 the commonwealth of Spook Erection was running just under 30 markets and Keith was responsible in one way or another for 17 of them. Then in 1978, disaster struck.

Chapter 8

Stormy Weather Home and Abroad -
1978 to 1981

On the 3rd of January 1978 a storm with tornadoes caused 136 geese caught up in it to fall dead from the sky and around the 11th and 12th Margate pier was destroyed. There were freezing fogs in the south and battering blizzards in the north. Some people were trapped in their cars for three days in drifts up to 6m deep in places where blizzards blew across Scotland at the end of that month.

The North Sea flood that January also caused considerable damage on the east coast of England. Severe flooding occurred in Lincolnshire, the Wash, north Norfolk and Kent, and piers along the east coast of England suffered severe damage.

As much as January was wet, stormy and cold, February in 1978 was freezing as an anticyclone from Scandinavia brought snowy and icy conditions with seriously low minus temperatures to most of the U.K. Exeter and Cardiff had 8m drifts, Newcastle had 30cms of snow and it also fell over much of the south and the midlands.

The great south west blizzard of the century
even hit Devon badly and many places were cut
off and lives were lost. In England, Keith and
his fellow Spook personnel were ordered by
their general manager, John Scarbrook, that
they must reach the markets in their charge. At
Newport in Wales they found seven-foot snow
drifts after a 14-hour drive. Impossible to clear,
the market site soon had four feet of snow and
no public access. Next, they set out for Bristol
and on the way there, their vehicle had a
radiator problem they had to repair with quick
drying cement to do until they returned home.

All the Spook markets were closed that
weekend and Keith and his teams battled
against the snow trying to clear all the sites he
was responsible for.

Later, in Scotland, where Braemar had frozen at
-21C on the 15th, as did Edinburgh at -17C on
the 17th of February, the temperature dropped
to -22C in the Grampians. The March winds
came howling in to Ingliston and the market
was destroyed.

Keith and his co-worker Fred Walker, worrying
about these conditions, spent the night at
Ingliston in a company van where they
witnessed the complete destruction of the
market site during that stormy weather. Some

stalls were blown miles away and the 800-stall market was very quickly destroyed.

Fred Walker was so distraught by the destruction, half way through the night he went up to the residential caravan he was staying in and packed his bags. Resigning there and then, he left Keith to cope alone.

When the weather cleared Keith rounded up a temporary labour force to clear up Ingliston and some extra stalls were mustered up from Moreton but the market was reduced from 800 stalls to only eight stalls, temporarily. Keith was Superintendent of Ingliston at this point in time and was worried this storm would close Ingliston for good.

Nigel took action. He sent out a letter to every one of the 800 stall holders explaining how Keith had had to make the decision on Sunday 19th March 1978 that Ingliston was a danger to the general public and would have to be closed until further notice.

This unfortunate act of God conflicted with Nigel's Spook Erection rules that stated both traders and Spook Erection personnel must attend their market businesses through, "snow, rain, hail, frost, mist, normal winds and even severe heat, should we have the pleasure of such an entity", as these did not constitute reasonable closure because, "they are presumable only being inflicted upon British Market Traders that became such after having knowledge of the climate of the British Isles and should therefore be prepared in every respect for the same."

He expressed in his letter how serious his company was taking this unfortunate series of events and stressed that the company "will continue to operate upon your behalf with the same sincerity and severity that we have done in the past whether it be when trade for you is extremely good or diabolically bad, kipper or burster."

With particular regard to the weather, and because of Ingliston's great potential, Nigel put a great deal of planning into getting the site moved to a better place, better prepared for poor weather conditions. Thousands of tons of red core, known as "blaze", once shale mined for paraffin, were delivered to lay a hard surface over the grassy site, at first. It had been mined locally and its slag heaps are known to this day as the "five sisters". It caused a lot of dust though so through time a new surface of tarmac was laid.

The promotional team at the head office in Moreton set to work, and Keith and his excellent workforce soon got the stalls re-erected. Nigel celebrated and rewarded their hard work once the tarmac was fully laid covering the whole site with a champagne breakfast onsite. Next, Nigel put on coaches to bring the public to the traders, true to his word and before long Ingliston was back up and running. By December 1978 when Keith was Market Manager, Ingliston had peaked at a massive 3,000 units! It was the biggest open-air market in the U.K., perhaps the world.

Nigel had also continued to invest his time and money into other new sites I Scotland and, for example, in June 1977, The Airdrie and Coatbridge Advertiser was reporting that Spook Erection, operators of "the world's largest open-air market at Ingliston" were to open a £100,000 market in Airdrie. They were already running a market there at Garlea Road, that Fred Walker had been in charge of until he resigned, since 1973, but now this larger market would be sited at land being cleared by Spook Erection at Manse Place. Speaking for the company, Mr David Johnston said that they expected the market to open late summer and since it was seen as a long-term venture, the company had leased the land from Monklands District Council for a 20-year period.

After the resurrection of Ingliston, in 1980, Keith was promoted by Nigel to Regional Manager of England and Wales and he was

moved down to head office where he had less
of a personal touch with the traders and
workforce. Now, he was involved in the
management and running of the commonwealth
of Spook Erection. This fortunate turn of events
allowed Keith to purchase a beautiful
traditional thatched home named "Woodbine
Cottage" in Shipston-on-Stour.

Keith's duties included conducting rent checks
on the markets after trolling through the
Tobies' written reports and various figures
received from them. Neither the labour force
nor the rent men and their Tobies would know
what days Keith would be turning up to inspect
them.

The sizes of the spaces that traders took up
dictated the cost of their rents and if any of
them went over the allocated space, they would
have to pay extra rent, so Keith had to inspect
his markets sites regarding this. Going over the
13-foot limit and not paying the extra rent
could cause a trader to be barred from trading,
and these rules had to be implemented by
Keith.

Spook Erection were becoming so well known
as successful market operators across the
country that, by 1980, rivals began to surface.
Open-air markets were extremely popular with
the public and others wanted a slice of the pie.

One of the most successful markets in central England in 1981 ran by Spook Erection was Brownhills near Birmingham and just before Christmas that year, on November 27th 1980, the Walsall Observer was reporting that trouble had "flared up again" between rival traders at Brownhill Market.

The established Spook market had 400 stalls operating at Brownhills and the rival operators, Redmond Enterprises had set up a small market adjacent to Spook's divided by a makeshift chain. This chain had been apparently put up after a fence had been torn down. The previous week, the rival's market had been blocked off using vans and lorries, and even manure had been put down to stop customers straying to the "wrong" market.

Traders on Spook Erection market were angry because they felt that Redmond's were attempting to cream off their Christmas trade. Keith was quoted as saying, "Our market has been here for 10 years and during that time we have built up a good reputation and invested a lot of money making it a good market. These chaps leap in a Christmas to cream of the trade."

The action taken to get rid of their rivals included overnight vigilant watching of the site, taking down unofficial fencing and stalls, welding their rival's gates up, and flooding the rival's site with water from the nearby canal. After an altercation with Mr Redford, who ended up in the canal, the police were called. This led to Keith being fined £120, paid for by Spook Erection. The rivals soon gave up.

Rules, after weathering such storms at home an abroad, had to be put in place for both Spook personnel and traders whose numbers had grown along with the company's assets, so much so that Nigel began compiling a Spook Erection handbook for publication that would be useful to both, that eventually became known as the "Spook Manual". In the meantime, in February 1980, he created and introduced to his Managers, a league table that he wanted them to use to monitor the performances of their workers.

These weekly league tables listed the names of the workforce according to their work performance record. By November 1980, anyone who came bottom of the list received a warning letter. Initially this first letter was known as a letter of registration. If they remained there three weeks running, further disciplinary action was taken including another, second warning letter. However, after 15 weeks or three warning letters, they could be sacked. Each Manager had the responsibility of judging or assessing the endeavours of the workers on his team, and recording them on the league table weekly.

When this workers league table was introduced to Keith, he found that he simply could not agree to it. Try it as he might, he found it was unfair, unworkable, and difficult to operate. From 1980 to 1982 this league table caused animosity between Keith and his team of 23 fellow workers as he tried it - out bringing mistrust and paranoia into his team of operators.

Keith tried during that period of time to operate the league table system more fairly by deliberately rotating the bottom position among the men so that no man appeared three times, because for anyone who worked for the firm for less than a year, that could mean instant dismissal. Keith pleaded and argued with Nigel that the system was, to him, unworkable. He was driven demented by it as this was an assessment on submitted paperwork, not on physical duties. His workers were scattered across the country and there was no fair way of assessing their performances or endeavours. Nigel's response to Keith was shocking.

After the years of hard work and utter loyalty that he had given to Nigel Maby and his company, on the 19th of August 1982 Keith was sacked.

Chapter 9

The Social Force of Moral Obligation
1982

John D. Rockefeller Jnr., once said "every right implies a responsibility; every opportunity, an obligation; every possession, a duty." All three of these senses demands a course of action that must be taken when considering right and wrong and there is no force stronger than the social force of moral obligation.

On the day that Keith arrived home to his beautiful Woodbine Cottage after being dismissed from Spook Erection, he was indescribably shocked. In 1982, his job was his life and he thought his life was his job, and his future. So much so that it had become the first consideration in everything that he did. His loyalty to Nigel was more like brotherly love, and the commitment that he had given to Spook Erection because of that, especially to his fellow workers, worked well because Keith had a strong sense of right and wrong. His sense of moral obligation to those workers was stronger than his personal feelings even for himself and this was the force that gave Keith the strength

to challenge and fight the decision Spook
Erection had made to dismiss him.

He felt within every inch of his heart that the
reasoning and way of judging those who
worked at Spook Erection, according to Nigel
Maby's league table system, was just wrong…
wrong for himself and wrong for any
workforce. Keith sat and reflected.

First, he looked around his beautiful Woodbine
cottage at Station Road, Shipton-on-Stour. He
remembered how he could not wait to share the
joy of purchasing this lovely property with his
father Ronald, and his wife. This, his dream
home, represented his success in life thus far,
after all his hard work and difficult upbringing.
He absolutely loved it and its situation. He
only needed to pop out his front door and walk
a short way away to nip along to his local pub
to relax. He had settled in, and this was his first
own home.

Secondly, he thought about those whom he had
worked with. Returning to head office in
England when he was promoted to General
Manager of England and Wales, Keith had re-
connected with some of the lads he had
previously started out with. One of them was
George Wheeler, known to his friends as
"Tucker". It was Tucker who had introduced
Keith to a motor racing sport known as Banger.

This type of stock car racing was extremely popular, and still is today, and it took place on Sunday's and on Bank Holiday weekends. The perfect sport for the working man who loved driving.

As competitive as it was, it was also great fun for those involved, and as Keith reflected he realized it reminded him of the happy days he had spent with Ronald at the motorbike racing, and he thought about how Ronald was so proud of him now that he was doing a bit of racing.

Any type of car could be raced from a Jaguar right down to a mini, as long as it was stripped down to a bare shell and then rebuilt according to safety requirements. Tucker persuaded Keith to get involved and before long he found himself loading an old car on to a trailer carrying a multitude of spare parts including tyres etc., happily getting ready to travel to the circuit.

The popular circuits were Standlake, Westbury, Farrington and Newbury, and in his first season, Keith felt out of his depth. But his motto of "never give up" determined that he would work over the closed season on a lighter, smaller vehicle for 1981 and he and Tucker fitted it up perfectly. It was given the registration number of "MAD 99". Keith was proud as punch driving it for the first time at

90

Standlake. The perfect speed machine, once Keith mastered his drifting technique, the trophies began to build up over that season.

Then, in the 1982 season, another fellow worker, a woman, joined their team for the racing season, adding to their success. Keith collected over 40 racing trophies. After a full days racing, the happy team would gather together at the local pub to celebrate their success and continue the day's fun with a game of darts or cards.

Thirdly, he reflected upon all of the work he had done in his life to get where he was now. Throughout his childhood he had worked as soon as he was old enough. Even whilst was in the care of Mrs Pearce, he had worked clearing glasses at a nearby pub. He smiled at the memory of how he, just a young boy, had sneakily slurped on the left overs customers had left just to see what they tasted like… He remembered how he'd worked as a teenager seven days a week on his paper round and delivered shopping for the local green grocer to pay of the awful, never ending clothing account ran by his step-mother… How he'd escaped to the army, then started his full time civilian work in The Golden Egg as a chef… He remembered the first time he met Nigel and how far they had travelled together along the parallel roads of Spook Erection's growth and development. He thought about the last, exhaustive ten years he had put in for the company and about how it may just have reached its peak.

Over those ten years, Nigel had ruled his company with a rod of iron but Keith had formed a good opinion of him and admired the man. He understood where Nigel was coming from, but that didn't mean that he could always agree with some of the policies that he laid down.

He contemplated on the high standards of work that Nigel expected from his labour force and how those had helped the company prosper, but then he remembered how, if any member of the workforce whether management or labour was one minute late for work, he would be sent home and lose that day's pay. Keith, himself, had fired many people over that past ten years who had fallen foul of the company's policies, and he had sent them home too after implementing the one-minute late rule. He thought about them now after losing his own job.

He considered the Spook Erection Manual, and where it could be improved. Keith agreed with the manual in principle, and with the rules and regulations of the company being written down for all to see and to understand... but therein lay the problem. They were often difficult to understand as Nigel had tried to write up guidance within his manual to cover every eventuality, which was impossible.

He pondered upon how the Spook Erection manual had become known quietly by all employees as, "Nigel's Baffler" and why. All the employees from the general managers to the dustcart driver had to sit a written examination at a seminar that was held at the Tickled Trout Hotel in Preston, Lancashire. This exam lasted for around three hours and the papers were marked right there and then. Results were publicly announced and read out leaving some very red faces!

Study of the Spook Erection manual had to be undertaken by each employee in their own time and after a twelve- hour shift and often working seven days a week, the wording of some of the sections of this enormous bible-sized manual became difficult to understand... and yet studying it was their only way of making themselves familiar with all aspects of the company.

Such tough rules had often led Keith into conflict with traders both emotionally and physically and he thought about that now. He was once confronted by a trader with a carving knife for giving his pitch away on Wishaw market, where he was superintendent at the time. Keith had given away the pitch because the trader hadn't turned up and no goods were displayed by opening time. The Spook Erection rules clearly stated that a pitch had to be allocated to another trader in such cases. After pulling a knife, of course that particular trader lost his pitch forever!

Keith reflected upon a number of disputes that he had encountered and had to deal with over the company's policies. He had been threatened with dress rail bars, involved in punch ups between traders over distances allowed for pitches and/or allocations. He had chased after shoplifters, policed grounds for the company in case of rogue traders and he'd even landed up in conflict with the law when standing with, and by, Nigel's principles.

But now these rules had come back and bit Keith himself, all the happy recollections and successes he thought of also revealed the many injustices he had seen and the league table Nigel had imposed upon the managers and the labourers was a step too far.

Finally, after many hours of reflecting, hurting, emoting, and mulling over his previous ten years working for Nigel at Spook Erection, Keith decided it was time to act. His instincts had told him that this league table was wrong from the start. He was now going to turn his frustration, hurt, and anger into something positive by fighting the injustice being inflicted upon the workforce at Spook Erection.

Acting accordingly Keith soon contacted Citizen's Advice. There, someone advised him that he could take Spook Erection to an unfair dismissal tribunal, and they gave him a list of solicitors who could help him. This helped his determination even more. Knowing he was in the right, he felt he could not lose.

Chapter 10

"Get up, stand up, Stand up for Your Rights", Bob Marley. 1983

On Monday January 10th 1983 Keith found himself in sitting in the Gloucester Crown Court with his solicitor Michael Peckitt in attendance of the first day's proceedings for his case against Spook Erection for unfair dismissal. The atmosphere, for Keith, was pretty intense as he found himself face to face with Nigel Maby who attended in person along with his legal representative, Mr McVitie. But Keith kept his nerve along with his confidence and conviction.

The court heard how the labour league table was a system designed by the company to assess the endeavours of the 25 labourers in England on a weekly basis. The system operated separately in Scotland and in Wales and in England it was under Keith's remit, wherein the managers had the responsibility of scoring each man on a table from 1 to 25 according to their assessment of that man's performance that week. The question being asked by the tribunal was: Was it reasonable to expect the foremen to undertake such a task?

After trialing the system from February 1980, the court heard how John Scarsbrook and Nigel Maby decided to make this table system a little more effective in 1981 by introducing warning letters for those who were consistently at the bottom of the league, and if an employee's name appeared at the bottom of the list 15 times within an 8 month period they would be dismissed. Mr McVitie described these events to the court and the chairman of the Tribunal could not hide his disapproval of the league table in reaction so, Keith was hopeful.

Nigel Maybe was examined and cross examined by Keith's solicitor and the court heard how Keith, after at first trying to operate the labour league table, had resolutely refused to when the system was changed and so he was therefore dismissed. After further discussions the case was adjourned until February 28th, 1984.

When the court resumed in February, Nigel was the first to give his evidence. He explained to the court that he had wanted to keep a regular file on each manager's observations about his workforce and that the labour league table was not a "sacking system" as Michael Peckitt, Keith's solicitor, had claimed. Mr Peckitt had suggested that Spook Erection were a 'hire and fire' company to John Scarsbrook, which

Scarsbrook denied. Keith said in evidence that he had told management of his disapproval of the idea of such a league table when he was first told about it and when the new system to the table was introduced he had ensured that no man's name would appear three times at the bottom of the unfair table.

The Tribunal resumed on April 30th 1983 at Tewkesbury Court, for final deliberations. That day, Keith's solicitor assured him that things were going reasonably well, so far. Michael Peckitt was a good solicitor and he had presented Keith's case professionally and appropriately, though it was an unusual case to say the least.

Keith had just returned from Scotland after a reunion with Theresa and his children in Glasgow. He had given her an update on the Tribunal's proceedings and had reassured her that things seemed to be going well. During this period of time, Nigel had offered Keith his job back twice, and they had met outside of the Tribunal, but because Nigel would not get rid of his awful league table, Keith felt he had to stand up for both his rights and the rights of the men at Spook Erection, so he kindly refused his offers.

Both of these men had given most of their living hours to the markets they had created and they had worked very closely together over the years. Keith respected Nigel as a mentor too and he did not dislike him. Nigel did not dislike Keith either. This whole disagreement was over a system that Nigel could not see was unfair and unjust and he stubbornly determined that the league table would remain as company policy along with the Spook Erection manual of rules he had compiled.

Financially Keith was starting to struggle. His determination to win his case was costing Keith a lot and one newspaper even reported that Keith would probably have to pay in excess of £1,000 alone for legal the expenses to simply complete his case. He was now carefully considering setting up his own market business, depending on what the outcome of this Tribunal would be.

The chairman of the Tribunal, Mr Peter Williams announced the Tribunal's decision. He said, "One cannot, in our view, assess the endeavour of employees through the agency of a foreman who sees them but infrequently during the week. To attempt to compare the endeavours of men operating different skills in that way is, in our view, impossible and any findings are meaningless". But, he said the system was not unlawful and that Keith could not claim it incapable of being operated because he had done it for two years. Mr

Williams continued, "Accordingly, with regret, we feel obliged in the light of the law as it now stands to dismiss the complaint".

As a triumphant Nigel left the Tribunal with his solicitor, Keith sat still absolutely stunned. He was shocked, hurt and angry. It seemed as though the members of the Tribunal agreed with everything he had felt about the awful labour league table yet they had dismissed his case because the table was legal?

Keith stepped up. He discussed with Michael Pickett the possibility of a review against the Tribunal decision. Mike advised him that it was possible, but costly, so Keith instructed his solicitor to go ahead and get some sort of appeal going. He would find the money somehow. He remembered his own motto to never give up and thinking it over and over he wasn't going to.

After returning to his dream home, Woodbine Cottage, Keith took a good look around, nostalgically thinking of how proud he was of it when he first picked up the keys after arranging the mortgage for it. Now, he thought, it would have to go, He would have to let go of his beloved cottage and everything in it in order to finance his corner. A hard decision, but the best one in the circumstances.

After the sale of the cottage, he auctioned off
his furniture to a local saleroom in July 1983,
and then he moved in with his friends Tony and
Veronica Molyneux at Preston, Lancashire.

The following month, Keith set up his own
market company business entitled, "Universal
Markets", indirectly funded by two of his
colleagues who were working for Spook
Erection at the time. However, funds were
insufficient as Keith was struggling financially
with the bulk of his money going towards legal
fees and costs.

In January 1984, Keith's solicitor Mike Pickett
was unsuccessful in an attempt to obtain a
review of Keith's failed tribunal. To take it any
further, Keith would now need not only a
solicitor but a Q. C., to attend an Employment
Appeal Tribunal case in London. By this time
Keith was actually unemployed and filled with
uncertainty. He felt so wrapped up in failure,,,
but he was determined to break out. Being out
of work he was claiming unemployment
benefit. Having so much time on his hands, he
was aware that he'd been spending more of it in
his local drinking and eating there. He'd even
put on weight and that didn't make him feel
healthy... The pressure was certainly on.

Even with all of this pressure, Keith felt
determined every time he thought of Nigel's

labour league table and how it should be stopped. If it was legal, then it shouldn't be, because it was unfair and unjust. Keith pondered over Nigel's rules and remembered how once, when every employee was working long hours for Spook Erection, the company found itself short of workers. A young man had once come into Keith's office looking for work and Keith was very glad to see him. He was over 21, married, but his wife was eight months pregnant, so Keith took him on as they were so short of labour. Just a couple of weeks later Nigel had turned up at the yard and when he saw the lad he got into a conversation with him. As soon as he found out the young man's wife was pregnant he told him he was out of a job and to come back after his wife had given birth!

Then Nigel stormed into Keith's office to give him a rollicking for taking on someone who did not meet the firm's criteria. The young man was sitting at the bottom of the stairs crying, an unfortunate victim of Nigel's mad rules.

Sometimes in life we reach what feels like rock bottom but when we land there, the only way is up and Keith's strong sense of right and wrong gave him the strength he needed to fight on. If something wrong is legal, then it ought to be outlawed and Keith was on the right side of history. He and his solicitor pressed on and an appeal was fixed to be heard on the 16th of February, 1984, at 4, St. James' Square, London.

Chapter 11

"What's Past is Prologue," William Shakespeare. 1984

The media coverage of Keith's case against Spook Erection had brought about a lot of attention to both Keith and Nigel. To Nigel, all publicity was as good as advertising for his growing company, but personally he preferred privacy. At the beginning of 1984 he had retreated to his home office in Scotland after the Christmas break a troubled man.

Reflecting upon the whole saga of Keith's dismissal, Nigel hadn't banked upon Keith's strength of character. He realised now that Keith wasn't just being stubborn, he was truthful, and right. How had Nigel finally come to this conclusion?

With some fascination Nigel had been monitoring the media reports about the case against the company for 18 months when, at the end of 1983, after Keith's defeat at the tribunal, he had opened the Market Magazine to discover that Keith had taken up his pen to give that particular magazine and exclusive series of articles about his ten years employment with his company, Spook Erection. Throughout

December 1983, a mesmerised Nigel had both smiled and wept as he read Keith's copy eagerly, which told of their times together. In the last in the series the Market Magazine had quoted Keith saying, "In one way I am sorry that I am no longer working for that company. I enjoyed working for Nigel." Nigel remembered how he had offered Keith a job in the first place, and why.

Keith meantime, nervous about the forthcoming Employment Appeal Tribunal due to assemble on the 16th February, 1984, was busy in the local library researching the history of markets for another series of articles he was writing for publication in the Market Magazine. It was entitled, "The Origins of Markets and Fairs."

On the evening of the 15th February, 1984, Keith found himself boarding the overnight coach to London to attend his appeal tribunal the next day. Arriving in Victoria Bus Station about six thirty in the morning of the 16th, after a restless and uncomfortable journey with very little sleep, Keith decided to have a shower in the station. He was robbed whilst showering of his watch and silver bracelet, and this prompted a mood of dread within him. He had no money either.

He walked from the bus station to St. James' Square where he met his Q.C. Mr James

Watson for the first time, then he took up his seat inside the court to listen to the hearing. It lasted a full day and Keith was very pleased with Mr Watson's performance, though he could see, and noted, that Spook Erection's solicitor Mr McVitie was not comfortable with the day's proceedings. The case finished in the late afternoon and it was decided that judgement would be given on the case shortly at a later date. Keith headed back to the station to catch the overnight bus back to Preston.

Meanwhile Nigel Maby had decided he wanted Keith back, and offered Keith a staff position. Lack of money and responsibility for himself and his family preyed on Keith's mind. Should he go back after all that had happened? Fred Coutts thought he should, at least until Keith had set up some markets of his own... Keith was so fed up hitch-hiking between Scotland and England to visit Theresa and his children and his father Ronald, having his own transport again certainly appealed to him, but there was no way Keith felt he could return to Spook Erection unless the league table was removed...

Quicker than expected, Keith's solicitor Mr Peckitt called, on the 28th of February to say the judgement was going to be announced the next day, on the 29th February, 1984, a leap year day. The result was imminent, but Keith could not afford to travel down for it. His good friend Tony, whom Keith was still staying with, couldn't afford to lend him any money to go down to London either. Mr Peckitt would attend.

The next day Keith signed on at the Employment Office in Preston in the morning and occupied himself in the main library to continue his research and take his mind of the proceedings that he knew were going on in London. After about five hours there, he returned to Tony's home to wait for Mr Peckitt's call. It was great news! The judgement had not only gone in his favour but Keith had changed history. The judgement was set in stone and the league table would have to go. Spook Erection had lost their case and would now have to update their system.

After 18 months of struggling, Keith had suffered frustration, inconvenience, and even been victimised for standing up for what was right. Winning his case against Nigel's company, he felt, made it all worthwhile. His motto of "Never give up," had seen him through.

Just three months later Keith found himself sitting in a meeting in the Head Office in Moreton-in-Marsh agreeing terms for his re-employment with Spook Erection. It was agreed with Nigel that Keith would return on the 2nd April, 1984, as a staff member, in Scotland, in the company's legal department known as SPAN, with continuity of employment from his original date of 7th February, 1975. A settlement was agreed to be paid in monthly installments to Keith's solicitor and a press release would announce, "It is announced that the Industrial Tribunal Proceedings between Keith Payne and Spook Erection Limited have been settled by mutual agreement and the proceedings are to be/have been withdrawn."

Mutual respect between Keith and Nigel remained. After staying with his friends Tony Mollyneux and his wife and three boys for 18 months, Keith could finally return home to Theresa and his children in Glasgow, triumphantly! He could not wait to see them.

Nigel had opened his own legal department which was based outside Edinburgh and Keith would now be based there in his new job. This department was known as the Spook Surveying, Planning and Negotiating Department, otherwise known as SPAN. Keith's new job consisted of travelling around the country looking for new market sites which, when discovered, he would create business proposals for Spook's lawyer and discuss those with Nigel. He was now living out of a suitcase again, and eating and sleeping in hotels and bed and breakfast establishments, this wasn't the same as being involved with the actual markets...

Keith was finding his new job tedious. Quite soon afterwards though, he was able to move his wife Theresa and their children from Glasgow to West Lothian to begin this new chapter of their lives.

Far away, in the West Midlands meanwhile, a young man named Kevin Roberts was dealing with the death of his father. He had always known he was adopted, but only now, after his father's passing in 1984, had he discovered that he had a brother named Keith and other siblings.

Earlier, in 1981, after the birth of his own daughter, Kevin had written to Dr Barnardo's to see help about how to recover his birth records and they had replied advising him to write to the offices of the General Registrar to find out exactly who to contact for the information about his early life. In 1984, Kevin was 28 years old and living with his wife and daughter when his adoptive father died. Once he found out he had a brother, he determined to look for Keith and he wasn't going to give up until he found him.

Shakespeare once wrote, "What's past is prologue," and he was quite right. Both Kevin and Keith having lived their joint prologues were about to discover their life stories.

EXCLUSIVE

Keith Payne's Scrapbook

Keith Payne has worked for Spook Erection and Nigel Maby almost from the very earliest days of the

Keith Payne's

The Origin of Markets and Fairs

Chapter 12

"When Time Changes, Light Shifts,"
Marilyn Reid. 1984 -1992

As Keith and Theresa settled into their new house in Livingston life was as hectic as ever for Keith. They now had a new addition to their own family, a little boy named Stephen Daniel, born at the end of 1984 just before they left Glasgow. Theresa, as always, the backbone of the family, looked after things at home independently and Keith hardly ever involved her in his decision making. He basically decided for her what she needed to be involved in when it came to his working life. He accepted that the home and family were her responsibility.

At this time, Keith still had his own company, Universal Markets, and he still toyed with the idea of going it alone because things were beginning to look a little shaky in the Spook Erection organisation. Nigel and his second wife, Diane, were separating and their divorce could mean the break up of the company.

Since taking up his new post at Spook Erection, Nigel had involved Keith in helping to compile and update the Spook Erection manual. In January's, at the time they called, "kipper season" when work was slow in the markets, Nigel would take some of his staff, including Keith, abroad to Tenerife to work on the administration of the markets the company had.

Nigel's behaviour, the staff noticed, was becoming more and more erratic and to them he was a loose canon. He not only wrote up, worked on constantly, he created the huge bible sized book, the Spook Erection manual, in sections. But now his rules included that twice a year his staff had to meet in Preston at the Tickled Trout Hotel for conferences where they would have to sit a 300 question test on the Spook Erection manual which covered every aspect of all three sections contained within it. Keith also noted how bizarre Nigel's actions were at those seminars. No-one knew then that Nigel Maybe was suffering from a brain tumour.

Out of the blue, Keith's sister Maureen called one day to tell him that their brother Kevin had been in touch. Incredulously, Keith didn't know that he had a little brother. He had literally forgotten Kevin. He was utterly shocked to hear this. Why on earth had no-one ever mentioned Kevin before? Neither his sister Maureen, brother Malcolm, father Ronald nor his step-mother Alma, had mentioned Kevin after his adoption. When Keith heard that both he and Kevin had gone into care as children together into the council nursery no matter how hard he reached down into his memory he could not remember having his brother there with him. He now felt betrayed by all the adults in his family.

Childhood amnesia is recognised as a natural part of childhood for every child from two until four years. When children are separated from their parents the grief they suffer because of that separation is eased by placing siblings together as children support one another. Siblings help each other to adapt to new and frightening conditions and new surroundings. Separating siblings compounds the grief they feel and separating them after placement is traumatic for them. Siblings are children's first peer group, keeping them together creates a stable family connection and helps them to achieve their early developmental milestones. Split them up, and their development takes a wobble. This is what happened to Keith and Kevin after their separation for a period of time.

Both children had behaviour issues, tantrums, and emotional outbursts for a period of time after separation. Then, their childhood amnesia kicked in and they settled into life without one another, not even knowing that they had suffered such early emotional trauma.

Kevin's adoptive parents were very good to him and he had become a big brother to two younger sisters. He'd had a stable life and had always known he was adopted. He was happily married with a young daughter of his own when he found out that he had come from Shipton-on-Stour and that he still had family there that he did not know. He visited Ronald and his wife there and Ronald had taken him into the kitchen to talk to him privately about why he was adopted. But Ronald, as we noted earlier, was not able to discuss emotions easily, even more so now that he was older.

Keith and Kevin finally reunited when Kevin came up to Livingstone to meet Keith's family, with his partner Gail, in 1986. It wasn't until all the papers were finally recovered from the authorities and Kevin and Keith read through them, that they could understand what the grown ups in their family had gone through at the time they were sent to the residential nursery. The time of their mother's death had sent Ronald, Maureen, Malcolm, Keith and baby Kevin spiralling into the darkness of a heartbreaking crisis out of control. In grief, they were making decisions that no-one would wish to make.

Ronald's only way of coping eventually after Kevin's adoption was to not talk about it at all. It was just too painful. Just as he never spoke of the war like many who suffered in that terrible conflict he preferred not to talk about the horror of it all. Just as he never spoke of the death of their mother.

Seeing Keith and Kevin together for the first time in her home, Theresa could not fail to see how alike they were. Strange coincidences and synchronisations were discussed between them too, how they'd both become chefs at one time, for example. Kevin too had worked hard in the firm of Dunlop to become a Foreman there and he hoped to go into management eventually. In April 1989, Theresa gave birth to another son and she and Keith named him Jamie Kevin after his newly returned Uncle.

Kevin's return affected Keith emotionally very much. Somewhere deep inside he felt betrayed by his own family. He needed to get to the root of it all. Both he and Kevin shared all the written information they could find about themselves and they corresponded with the care services to get the papers that they had about their past placements.

Both men were affected by their enlightenment and became very unsettled at the end of the 1980s. They had been sent on an emotional roller coaster about their identities, one that only *they* could understand. Of course nothing could be done now, no... but they had to understand what had happened to them to understand themselves. Knowing who you are is so important to one's identity and to discover that you have gaps in that knowledge can bring up uncomfortable truths. This emotional journey was a very tricky ship that sailed them through a sea of questions. However, truth is always best and as time changes light shifts. Reading Ronald's letters, written in his own handwriting, deeply moved them. The responses of the local childrens officers to Ronald's dilemma was very surprising to them both but after world war two Britain's social responsibilities were far different from where we see them today. Maureen helped them by providing photographs and information in so far as she knew it to be correct and this helped them very much, and Keith decided that one day he would have their family tree fully documented.

In 1992, Keith decided that he could no longer work for Nigel. He was attending one of Nigel's seminars at the Tickled Trout Hotel where staff were tested twice a year on the Spook Erection manual. Keith decided that he'd had enough, and he wasn't going to do the test. Of course, Nigel dismissed him... but Keith knew that would happen.

After Nigel's divorce Nigel's market empire had been demerged by the courts with Diane,

Nigel's ex-wife, being given the markets that he had set up and operated in Moreton-in-Marsh, Twekesbury, Carterton, Blackwood, Cinderford, Malvern, Newport and Bristol. This demerging of his company had had a bad effect on Nigel and he was also quite ill.

Nigel still had 16 other markets that Spook Erection were operating, every day except Wednesday, in England, and in Scotland where Ingliston market had reached its peak and was the biggest Sunday market in Europe.

Keith decided to resurrect his Universal Markets operating company. The future looked uncertain but he felt he must give it a try. Theresa was worried, but he hadn't even consulted her. She was also pregnant with their fifth child, Shaun Paul, who was born in March 1992.

Chapter 13

Spinning Too Many Plates 1993 - 1999

Guatama Buddha once said, "No-one saves us but ourselves. No-one can and no-one may. We ourselves must walk the path." Keith's new path was firmly established by September, 1993 and he was running his own markets under his company name of Universal Markets, but like a pool on a beach on a rainy day, his path was to become far rockier and slippier than he had anticipated.

Running his own markets successfully wasn't his first stumbling block. That was easy for Keith as his love for the market trade and his lifetime of experience had given him an expertise, second to none. He was very happy to be his own man and quite quickly he set up an indoor market in Broxburn on Thursdays, and two other indoor markets in Falkirk and Wester Hailes, as well as an outdoor/indoor market at Gayfield in Arbroath on the east coast of Scotland. He hadn't banked on dirty tricks from Nigel Maby, however.

The Courier reported, on Friday September 8th, 1993, how "local man Keith Payne's company had set up a weekly Thursday market in Broxburn next to the Regal Bingo hall in Greendykes Road" and that, "Mr Payne was annoyed that Spook had launched an attempted "spoiler" bus service the week before his market opened." Keith had explained to the reporter Frank Morgan that he was delighted by the response of the public during their first week of trading. Frank Morgan's headline though was entitled, "Market Wars Breaks Out", and his report exposes Nigel's intent.

Nigel's dirty tricks continued. Not only was he bussing people away from Keith's markets, he was asking traders not to trade at any of Keith's markets, especially if they wanted to continue trading at Spook Erection's markets.

Keith didn't have the financial clout or backing Spook Erection had accumulated, and he was finding it difficult to afford the staff he required to oversee his markets, taxing himself out trying to do so much of the work himself. Somehow, his markets were paying for themselves, but Keith could no longer afford the lifestyle his regular salary had given him previously, not could he afford to pay himself a huge amount or his staff, although he did hire part time staff. The burden of the responsibility of it all weighed heavily on him.

In 1995, when his step-mother Eileen died, Keith travelled down to Shipton-on-Stour to support his father Ronald. For a few years, Ronald had been taking care of Eileen at home. He had installed a hospital bed in the living room of their home when Eileen could no longer use the stairs, and he slept on the couch in the same room rather than upstairs in his bed, so that he could be there if she needed him. Keith was glad to be reconnecting with his father and so he went down to Shipton-on-Stour again about 18 months later to spend some time with Ronald.

It was then that he came to know more about his father's past. They took a trip down memory lane and visited Ronald's old haunts. Particularly pleasing for Ronald was their visit to Barton on the Heath where Ronald was born and brought up. He proudly showed Keith the drystane dykes he had built on the Barton estate whilst he'd been a stone mason there.

He also showed Keith the first house he had lived in with Keith's mother Kathleen when they were first married. It had had no running water at that time. A lovely young couple, owners of the same cottage at that time, were happy to allow them to look around at the improvements they'd made to Ronald's old home. The two men also visited the old churchyard where Kathleen was laid to rest not far from Ronald's little sister, and he told Keith that this was where he wished to be laid to rest himself, beside Kathleen. The following year Ronald passed away. It was 1999.

Keith was very grateful for the time he had spent with his father Ronald just before his died, but his passing brought much of Keith's past flooding back into his mind. Grief can bring up and out so many hidden traumas and Keith was also under stress and anxiety due to running his own business. Although he'd run very successful markets at Christmas, winter was really difficult for him. Rivalry from Spook Erection continued, with Nigel Maby threatening traders with losing their pitches if they traded on Keith's markets.

By the time of Ronald's death, Keith was already feeling desperately short of money and the winter drop in cash was not helping. Then he lost his market space at Falkirk to a new tenant, T.K. Max, and Arbroath made no money that winter either. His debts were growing... but another more

serious problem was also growing and developing... his consumption of alcohol. He was spinning too many plates and they were about to come tumbling down.

Chapter 14

The Abyss. 1999 - 2019

By the time Keith went down to help clear out his father's house in 1999, after Ronald's passing, he was already a heavy drinker. His alcoholism had been creeping up on him, unnoticed, since he'd worked as a boy at a hostelry near his foster mother clearing glasses. Whilst doing this after school job, young Keith had thought it funny to take a slurp out of the drinks left by customers... He had continued drinking regularly ever since. Working hard and playing hard for his generation generally included the reward at the end of a busy day, of a few drinks, "to wind down".

After Ronald's death, Keith was also drinking at home every night, Theresa noticed. He would justify it as his reward, but by then this habit had not only changed his personality, it had changed his sleep pattern, his decision making, and it was affecting his physical and mental health.

By 2000, Keith had only his Wester Hailes market left and even then he would sometimes stay off work. The Sheriff

Officers were about to arrive for his non-payment of council tax and he'd fallen behind on the mortgage payments for his house. Theresa could not take anymore and she and their two youngest sons, left Keith and went to live with Keith Jnr., and his girlfriend.

When the house was repossessed by the bank Keith moved into his car with some black bags packed with his belongings. He had fallen into the abyss. Now homeless, he had not only lost his home, he had lost his family too.

Identifying oneself as an alcoholic is difficult for most people and many do not realise the negative consequences of the drinking for a very long time. Tell tale signs like needing a drink to cope with stress or problems should alert someone as to the severity of their problem. Craving a drink regardless of where or what one is doing is another sign of uncontrollable addiction.

Keith, after losing everything and everyone, barely over his father's death, crashed emotionally. Life no longer making sense to him. He cried his heart out then, in his car, just as he'd done in the nursery after Kevin was taken away, all those years before. He broke down. It was then he decided to visit his G.P.

Fortunately Keith's G.P. was able to tell him that his body, physically, could still recover from his alcoholism and he advised him to get some rest and go to Alcoholics Anonymous for help to stop drinking. Al-Anon have safe places to talk and share experiences and they are a great source of support for anyone struggling with alcoholism. After contacting the A.A. helpline, Keith attended a meeting at Craigshill where he received the hand of friendship, just when he felt he was falling further into the abyss of terror, bewilderment and despair.

Keith kept going to the A.A. meetings while keeping his only market going at Wester Hailes and he went on to the A.A's step 12 program. The less he drank, the less his racing thoughts distracted him and he began to think more clearly and sharply about where he should be going with his life. It was clear to him that he'd tried to take on too much. He had to get back on track, but in a manageable way. His debts had to be tackled first, so after finding a single room in which to live in Livingstone, Keith registered for bankruptcy.

Not long after, he applied for the vacancy of General Manager of Kinross market and he was successful in getting that position. This helped his self esteem no end and he knew he could manage Kinross, with a good team around him. Keith was on the way up again, one step at a time. He persuaded his bank to open a basic account for him in order to receive his wages. Then, on 28th August 2001 came the day of Keith's redemption. He never touched alcohol again after that.

Six months after working in Kinross, Keith was able to move into a flat in Livingstone and he was quite settled working in that market doing what he'd always enjoyed the most, being a market man. He let Wester Hailes go in 2002 and he continued attending A.A. meetings and living life guided by the 12 steps.

In 2004, Nigel Maby passed away and just one year later Ingliston market was given up. It was reported that the site was to be used to extend Edinburgh Airport. Keith was shocked to hear of Nigel's death, Nigel was only 58 years old when he passed over with a brain tumour and people understood then why his behaviour had become so eratic. With affection and brotherly fondness, Keith put any differences he and Nigel had had behind him and paid his respects publicly to Nigel saying, "It was with great sadness that I heard of Nigel's passing. We went back many years, Having known him for over 30 odd years, I came into his employment way back in 1971.

Being a fresh faced 18 year old little did I know I was in for an interesting roller coastal journey, extending over many years. Like Nigel, I too was from the Cotswold village of Moreton-in-Marsh. I quickly became part of the ever -growing Spook squad and, through Nigel's guidance and leadership, I learned the arts of the workings of the general retail markets industry. In those very early days, we were like trailblazers, forging our way through uncharted territory, entering the unknown, en-route coming into contact with officialdom and, in many cases, beating them at their own game.

The Spook journey was to lead us to Scotland. Myself and another lad, having built 120 stalls. Nigel flying up for the opening day, we opened Ingleston Sunday market on 1st July 1973. The sheer size and scale of Ingliston was a sight to see. From the initial launch of 120 stalls, passing the 1,000 mark by 1975, growing in an ever upward direction, reaching the magical figure of 2,787 stalls. In today's rental figures that would equate to a daily income of £90,000. Some achievement from a former pig farmer and household linen trader! The rest, they say, is history." Keith felt he would always be grateful for what he had learned both in and out of Spook Erections employment, and for the part Nigel played in his life.

Well into his recovery, Keith was in the news again when he accepted a Piracy Award for Kinross market. Reconnecting with his family was his greatest goal and when Keith's daughter asked him to have a day out with her and her boyfriend he was pleased as punch. On that day out Anna Marie told her father they were to be married and that she wanted her father, Keith, to give her away. Keith could not have felt happier or prouder.

Just after discussing with the owner of Kinross a plan for a car boot sale there, the owner Alex Smith passed away and its ownership passed to a consortium. This consortium asked Keith to attend one of their meetings only to inform him that they would be lowering his salary and that he'd be getting a new, not so good, contract from them...

Luckily, one of Keith's old friends from Spook erection, Andy Bennett, offered him a position in Liverpool working for a French company named Jerome Markets. Keith left Kinross after almost seven years running Kinross market to take up his new position in Liverpool.

This job turned out to be a disaster as it was, "run by a gang of sharks and robbers". Keith informed his friend Andy Bennett about what was going on and headed back to Scotland. Whilst there he noticed and advertisement for a Market Manager in Manchester, in the market trade paper. He applied and became Market Manager of Gorton Indoor market which was opened six days a week, and the Manchester Wholesale Fruit and Vegetable Sunday market. As the head of markets development, Keith looked after a chain of markets around Manchester City. These were similar to farmers' markets. He made such as success of his work there he was awarded the Williamson Trophy in 2011.

But destiny had a different plan for Keith. Morris Leslie, a business man from Perth and Kinross in Scotland, saw and read the article about Keith's award and he was so impressed he sent one of his representatives, Mike McWilliams, down to Manchester to offer Keith the job of Market Manager at his Sunday market and car boot operation at Errol, Perth and Kinross. Together, after several meetings, the two men put together a business and investment plan for Errol market which has proved to be a great success ten years on. Errol market, at the time of writing, has a foot fall of 10,000 visitors, most weeks for the year, and is still growing into a huge enterprise for a new generation of traders.

In an interview Keith gave about the success of Errol Market, in 2019, Keith was asked about his ambition and he replied saying, " I would like to achieve a golden 50 year continuous service to this incredible and wonderful industry, which would mean retiring at the age of 68 in July, 2022."

Keith's motto of "never give up" helped him to get himself back out of the abyss and into the market trading world he loved and in 2021 he celebrated his 10th anniversary of service at Errol market and in 2022 he was made a Director of Morris Leslie's company. He had reached his 50 years continuous service. Now a happy family man and grandfather, life had treated Keith very well indeed for the those ten years and he had worked so hard to achieve resurrecting his life, but fate had just thrown Keith his greatest challenge.

Chapter 15

The Great Beyond. 2022 - 2023

When the great beyond beckons we may never be ready for that last journey on the path of life, and some of us may never know we've reached it. Of course we all will reach it, but for those who have an inkling that their path is leading there, the chance to reflect on what they have done with their life, and may still do now, is a great gift to some.

Keith is one such man. The journeys of life that we have taken with him whilst reading this, his biography, have taught us that he makes things happen, that he is capable of turning bad into good. That we too, must never give up, and Keith's life teaches us how truth, no matter how hard, must be faced if we are to make something good happen. He is an inspiring human being to us all. This chapter presents Keith's biggest challenge introduced by him in his own words, as he turns it into something good.

"As difficult as this is, I have taken the decision to share my Cancer journey with

you to create awareness, and in the hope that you will get behind me to raise as much as possible for my chosen charities. It won't change my outcome, but it can make a difference for so many others...

Let's start from the beginning. My relationship with Cancer, otherwise know as the 'Big C' began some time ago with developing symptoms back in January 2021. After many tests, scans, and diagnostics, in March 2022 my verdict was in. Advanced Gastric Cancer and Prostrate Cancer.

I was to discover and quickly realised that this terrible disease has no conscience whatsoever. It will attack anyone irrespective of sex, age, race, financial status, social standing or religious belief. After the diagnosis my thoughts moved to, 'Treatment', I can beat this! Sadly, not. I found myself in the desperately sad situation of having to accept that there were no treatment options available to extend my life and especially in the case of Gastric Cancer.

'Why me? Poor me,' followed the devastating consultation that left me overwhelmed with sadness, bringing lots of different fears, emotions and tears.

However the professionalism of the NHS team from their care to understanding and even the equipment used has been and outstanding and comforting experience.

My wonderful family, my wife along with children - my five diamonds... have and continue to give me truly fantastic support. Because of them, and mentally being a very much strong-willed individual not wishing to let the world pass me by, and most certainly having no desire whatsoever of becoming a couch potato wallowing in self pity, I quickly pulled myself out of this negative state of mind, accepting that 'Teamwork makes the Dream Work', and that every day is a precious gift, hence I chose to continue working within and industry that I have been a part of for more than 52 years.

Today as I continue to slide down life's helter skelter, I have made a conscious decision to go Public with my illness to generate awareness of this terrible disease, where early detection is key and certainly in the case of prostate cancer, is treatable. I know so many of you reading this will have your own experiences with Cancer whether personally or with family and friends.

If I can make a difference for others, I will, and that is why I would like to raise funds towards the wonderful work and ongoing research done by Cancer Research U.K., Prostate Cancer U.K., and Macmillan Cancer Support. I can't raise any large funds alone, however, but collectively, linking hands together to form an army, we can make something amazing happen when a lot of people donate a little.

I would be grateful for any contribution no matter how small, every penny counts. any funds raised will be split evenly between the above three charities and administered on my behalf by my two powers of attorney (my children), Look out for updates on events and sponsorship opportunities as me and my team make plans to raise this goal to £15,000, so I can give back just a little.

My final word of advise to you all, my friends, should you for whatever reason feel unwell, please speak to your G.P."

The above story is the one that Keith wrote when he launched his fund raising appeal on behalf of the three charities noted above. The aim was to give each of them £5,000 each, and that seemed like a huge and daunting task at the launch in Spring of 2023.

But help was at hand, and Lee-Ann Wilson, one of Morris Leslie's marketing team helped Keith to draw up a fundraising plan, it was named the Keith Payne Big C and Me appeal. What a success!

From sky dives to baking sales, collection buckets to auctions, and entertainment nights, Keith's colleagues, market traders and stall holders, family and friends, have linked their hands together forming Keith's visionary army. He has been "blown away" by the success and has raised over £30,000 for these named charities, and another favourite of Keith's, CHAS, will also receive £5,000.

Lee-Ann, who has supported Keith every step of the way on his charitable path said, "Keith's friends were honoured to be able to return the years of loyalty, support and friendship he had shown to them. "From the beginning, Keith said that alone he could only do so much. But together, with his families, friends and colleagues by his side, we would form an army and make great things happen. And that is exactly what we have done. Keith gave us an opportunity to channel our sadness into something positive and we have been inspired to help him reach his goal."

People who have known Keith in the past have been inspired by him, and he is still inspiring those of us who know him today, because he makes things happen by living life to the full, and caring for humanity. He is alive and sparkling and there is no doubt that his shining light will affect those who read this, his life story, in a loving, inspiring, positive way.

All Royalties from the sale of this book are going to The Big 'C' Bank Account to be shared between Keith's four charities, Prostate Cancer, Cancer Research UK, Macmillans, and Children's Hospice Across Scotland, (CHAS).

If you would like to make a further donation please send it to:-

Royal Bank of Scotland, Keith Payne, Sort Code: 83-06-08
Account number 21356428.

Errol's 'Mr Market' turns
cancer diagnosis into a £3
for good

When Errol Sunday Market director Keith Payne learned
he set his mind to helping others.

PREMIER SUNDAY MARKET

THE BIG C CARBOOT S
£1325.5
RAISE
£34,181.53 RAISED IN T(

THE
BIG
C
AND ME!

EPILOGUE

In March of 2023, when Keith took the decision to share his battle with terminal cancer to raise public awareness and fundraise for Prostate Cancer U.K., Macmillan Cancer Support and Cancer Research U.K., he knew he had to link arms with his amazing army of friends and family to make amazing things happen. At the time of the completion of this book, he had raised just under £35,000, a truly incredible figure.

Despite his ill health, Keith to date, November 2023, rarely misses a market at Errol and to his team and traders his is a market champion. So much so, that, unknown to Keith, two of his colleagues, Andrea and Fraser had submitted his name as a possible candidate for the prestigious award of Life Time Special Achievement to the General Retail Industry, to be presented at the Conventions Gala Dinner Dance and Award which all three of them were attending 9th to 10 October 2023. To their pride and delight, Keith, Market Director of Errol Sunday Market, was selected to receive this award. He was both bowled over and humbled by this incredible recognition.

N.A.B
.M.A,
the
Natio
nal
Asso
ciatio
n of
British Market Authorities, who presented
Keith with his award said they were proud
to share the celebration of Keith's more
than 50 years continuous service in the
industry, by presenting him with this award
of Special Achievement for his bravery and
for his inspiration as a true market
champion, and to say thank you to Keith for

sharing both his life of service and story of that life to help others.

The following words from Keith himself, upon reflection, at the closing of this book, will hopefully inspire all who read his story too.

"Reflection or hindsight is such a wonderful gift, and from a personal point of view, from the day we are born until the day we die, (it happens to all of us), it's the timeline in-between we all have to deal with. As we wander through our own personal highways and byways, each and every one of us have to confront Life's issues, dealing with them as best we possibly can. Sometimes easily, and at other times with great difficulty.

From my own personal life's experience I was to develop a strong line of character of 'Never Give Up' no matter what confronts us. I draw inspiration from Mother Nature, never looking downwards but turning one's eye-line to the abundant gift that lies before and around each and everyone of us.

Seeing and Breathing In this truly magnificent gift, Mother Nature gives me the total inspiration to deal with one day at a time. I trust and truly hope that my memoirs will enable you to 'Never Give Up' on your own life's journey."

Keith A. Payne, Author,

Never Give Up

My Life's Journey from the Markets to the Bic 'C' and Me

November 2023.

Editing, Narration, and Photographic imaging, cover and inserts, by Author/Illustrator Marilyn Reid of Artspixels Ltd., 1 Cumberland Close, Kirriemuir, Angus, DD8 4 EF, Scotland U.K. www.artspixels.uk